CH00726544

REFORMATION REBOOT!

THE NEED OF THE 21ST-CENTURY CHURCH

PAUL YEULETT

EP Books (Evangelical Press), Registered Office: 140 Coniscliffe Road, Darlington, Co Durham DL3 7RT

admin@epbooks.org

www.epbooks.org

EP Books are distributed in the USA by:

JPL Books, 3883 Linden Ave. S.E., Wyoming, MI 49548

order@jplbooks.com

www.jplbooks.com

© Paul Yeulett 2020. All rights reserved.

British Library Cataloguing in Publication Data available

ISBN 978-1-78397-279-1

Scripture quotations are from The ESV® Bible (The Holy Bible, English Standard Version®), copyright © 2001 by Crossway, a publishing ministry of Good News Publishers. Used by permission. All rights reserved.

This book is dedicated to the congregation of Grove Chapel, Camberwell, on the 200th anniversary of its founding in 1819.

I have consecrated this house that you have built, by putting my name there forever. My eyes and my heart will be there for all time.

— 1 KINGS 9:3

CONTENTS

ACKNOWLEDGMENTS

I am indebted to all those people who taught me about the Protestant Reformation, beginning with some of my teachers at school four decades ago, Monica Smale and James Tilly of The King's School, Ely. My special gratitude goes to John Gray, former teacher of Religious Education at Emmanuel College in Gateshead, who passed on to me my first copies of Merle d'Aubigné's *The Reformation in England*. Other erstwhile colleagues at Emmanuel College, in particular John Little and Jonathan Winch, inspired me to take up the reading of the Reformers and Puritans.

I will forever be grateful to the Lord for the influence and example of the late Brian Norton in Durham Presbyterian Church, for whom the godly reformation of the church was a lifelong concern. Brian's prayerful endeavours to secure the order and purity of the church continues to be a blessing to the congregations of the Evangelical Presbyterian Church in England and Wales.

Of all the many authors, pastors and godly saints who have encouraged me in this work, I would especially remember Iain Murray, my predecessor at Grove Chapel – with three other ministers in between! – whose own writings, and long-time involvement with the Banner of Truth, have made an impact on me and on countless others, which is probably impossible to measure.

My earnest thanks go to Graham Hind, who has given wholehearted support and encouragement throughout the preparation of this publication. He has been a stalwart help, patiently and persistently bearing with me while this book was being put together. I would like to add my thanks to all the staff and volunteers working for Evangelical Press, who have worked so thoroughly, and yet unobtrusively, to enhance this work as much as possible.

The majority of the chapters contained in this book are based on a series of sermons preached on Sunday evenings at Grove Chapel, in the autumn of 2017. I give thanks to God for his faithful people at Grove, who, like the early believers in Thessalonica, 'received the word of God' and 'accepted it not as the word of men but as what it really is, the word of God' (1 Thessalonians 2:13). On the occasion of Grove Chapel's bicentenary we have ample reason to give thanks and praise to God, who has faithfully fed his people here in Camberwell for so long. The Lord has built up a congregation of warm-hearted, encouraging and prayerful brothers and sisters, whom I value so much.

Finally, of course, I pay tribute to my wife Ruth, without whom, humanly speaking, none of this could ever have been attempted. She remains my closest and truest friend. I will also mention our children Rebecca, Matthew and Daniel, with a prayer that the God of the Reformation will continue to be their God, and the God who will work yet greater wonders in the generation to which they belong.

INTRODUCTION

The Protestant Reformation: an event that happened almost five centuries ago. How relevant is it today? Granted, there were commemorations in 2017 to mark the nailing-up of Martin Luther's 95 Theses, but this is 2020, not 2017, let alone 1517!

I studied the Protestant Reformation at school. Perhaps 'studied' is a little too flattering. More accurately, I *endured* those history lessons which covered the seemingly unending phenomenon called the Protestant Reformation. I enjoyed hearing about Henry VIII and how he beheaded two of his six wives. I remember the teacher being much more amused than the pupils were by the title of the 'Diet of Worms.' I struggled to spell 'transubstantiation,' before nearing any understanding of its meaning. No need to worry. Transubstantiation will not be mentioned again in this book. Neither will those worm pies or severed heads.

Fast forward to the summer of 1995. I was still in the classroom but, by now, I was standing at the front rather than sitting at a desk — a much happier place to be. On the last day of term, a senior colleague handed me a pair of hard-back books with imposing artwork emblazoned on the front and back covers, and told me: 'You should read these over the summer holidays. Every young Christian man should read Merle d'Aubigné on the Reformation.' The books were a gift, not a loan, and I began to read.

The title of the first chapter of the first book, 'Christ Mightier than Druid Altars and Roman Swords,' was stirring enough to accelerate my pulse-rate, and the words of the first paragraph still send a shiver down my spine:

> Those heavenly powers which had lain dormant in the church since the first ages of Christianity, awoke from their slumber in the sixteenth century, and this awakening called the modern times into existence. The church was created anew, and from that regeneration flowed great developments of literature and science, of morality, liberty, and industry. None of these things would have existed without the Reformation. Whenever society enters upon a new era, it requires the baptism of faith. In the sixteenth century God gave to man this consecration from on high by leading him back from mere outward profession and the mechanism of works to an inward and lively faith.[1]

The pages that followed were saturated with history — a history written with passion and vigour. The political exploits of kings and bishops ran side-by-side with the heroics of ordinary folk. It was not a local, little history either; it began in the distant mists of pagan Britain before spanning sixteen centuries. It was architectonic, panoramic, and altogether glorious. It reminded me of a view of the earth across many thousands of miles of outer space. In short, it was a page-turner. And it was a book on the Reformation!

The Reformation did not simply occur because Henry VIII's roving eye landed on a girl nearly twenty years younger than his middle-aged wife. It did not happen because Martin Luther had a few spare nails and a brand new hammer he wanted to try out. It did not even happen because a sixteenth-century version of Brexit suddenly swept across Europe. *The Reformation happened because God made it happen.* The God of heaven determined to visit his people and to return to them the greatest gift of all: the gospel of his Son, the Lord Jesus Christ.

How important is the Reformation? I would summarize like this:

- *Because of the Reformation*, we have Bibles in our own languages, to read from and to preach from.
- *Because of the Reformation*, we have a renewed and enhanced understanding of the gospel and of theology.
- *Because of the Reformation,* Europe was turned upside down religiously and politically.
- *Because of the Reformation*, we have a great deal more peace, freedom and democracy in our world than would be the case were it not for the Reformation.

- *Because of the Reformation*, we have the children of the Reformation: the great English Puritans, the Scottish Covenanters, the French Huguenots and the German Pietists. We also have the leaders of the Evangelical Awakening of the eighteenth century: George Whitefield and the Wesleys in England; Rowland, Harris and Pantycelyn in Wales; Jonathan Edwards in America; men like C. H. Spurgeon and J. C. Ryle in the nineteenth century, and others who have followed them since.
- *Because of the Reformation*, the worldwide missionary movement of the last two hundred years was born.

In 1995, I decided that I wanted to stand in the line of the Reformation, and (nearly a quarter of a century later) I still do. The Protestant Reformation was nothing less than a rediscovery of the 'faith that was once for all delivered to the saints' (Jude 1:3), the clear message that no one can be saved by their own efforts or by any outward ceremony, but only by faith in Jesus Christ — a crucified and risen Saviour. I love the Reformation because, at its heart, is the biblical gospel that the Lord Jesus gave to the apostles himself — the gospel that must be believed, if anyone is to know God and live for ever.

This book, however, is not a historical study. It mentions history from time to time, by way of illustration, but I really want to think about the timeless lessons, not of *the* Reformation as such, but of *reformation* in general. Why?

Because today, the church and the world desperately need another one. Perhaps God will give us another reformation. If he does, it would not be exactly like the one five hundred years ago. It will, however, share this in common — *it will bring us back to the gospel, and therefore back to the Bible.* For this reason this book focuses on the Bible. As a reader, you will need a Bible at your side rather than a Reformation wall-chart or timeline. Turn to Isaiah 17 and, having meditated on the discussion questions below, proceed to the first chapter.

Questions for discussion

1. Did you learn about the Reformation at school? Did your experience prejudice you against the subject, or excite your interest?

2. In 1916, Henry Ford wrote 'History is more or less bunk. It's tradition. We don't want tradition. We want to live in the present.' What do you think of his assessment in the light of what you have just read about the Reformation?

3. What other benefits do you think have come to the world as a result of the Reformation?

4. What do you think are the greatest needs of church and society? What kind of reformation are *you* praying for?

Chapter 1

LOOK TO OUR MAKER

> In that day man will look to his Maker, and his eyes will
> look on the Holy One of Israel. He will not look to the
> altars, the work of his hands, and he will not look on
> what his own fingers have made, either the Asherim or
> the altars of incense.

— Isaiah 17:7-8

Why do we need to say more about the Reformation?
Because apart from the Bible itself and the ministry of the
apostles recorded in its pages, no event has been so mighty,
so significant, or so influential in shaping the character of
church history and life — and indeed life and history
beyond the church — than the Reformation.

Whilst this is a grand claim, this book is not alone in its
proclamation. William Cunningham, Professor of Church
History at New College, Edinburgh, and then Principal
from 1847 to 1861, wrote these words:

The Reformation (from Popery) in the sixteenth century was the greatest event, or series of events, that has occurred since the close of the Canon of Scripture; and the men who are really entitled to be called the "Leaders of the Reformation" have a claim to more respect and gratitude than any other body of uninspired men that have ever influenced or adorned the church.[1]

Political correctness?

Cunningham did not adhere to political correctness. I agree with Cunningham's assessment without any reservation or hesitation. A great deal was said around the time of the five hundredth anniversary of the beginning of the Reformation about the great division, even the tragedy, caused by the Reformation. Harriet Sherwood, writing in *The Guardian* on 30 October 2016, reported that:

On Monday [31 October 2016] an ecumenical service led by Pope Francis at Lund cathedral in southern Sweden will herald a year of events running up to the 500th anniversary of the move that resulted in the greatest schism in western Christianity and a string of religious wars — and which has sectarian echoes today on the football terraces of northern Europe.

Christian leaders and congregations will spend the next 12 months consolidating moves towards greater cooperation and dialogue after centuries of division. In the first papal visit to Sweden in more than 25 years,

Francis will lead prayers asking "forgiveness for divisions perpetuated by Christians from the two traditions."[2]

Notice the language: 'schism ... wars ... sectarian ... division ... forgiveness'; this is, apparently, not something to be grateful about. Should we be sorry, ashamed and embarrassed about what happened in Europe in the sixteenth century?

Great historical movements — political, cultural, and industrial, as well as religious — are seldom completely 'clean.' It could be argued that a great deal of collateral damage was done in the wake of the Reformation, but it would not be fair to assign all the blame to the Reformation itself, as if fights between Rangers and Celtic fans were somehow the direct consequence of what the Reformers did centuries earlier.

If the Reformation was anything, it was a rediscovery of a dormant Bible which for many centuries had been kept away from the ordinary people, because it was imprisoned in the Latin language. Few of the priests, and even fewer ordinary people, could understand Latin. With the Reformation, the voice of God was heard again. This single achievement would have justified the Reformation, even if nothing else had arisen from it.

Mike Reeves summarizes the true essence of the Reformation:

Reformation occurs when the light of God's Word shines into places of spiritual and cultural darkness and transforms the people of God. This is why the motto of the Protestant Reformation became "After Darkness, Light" — *post tenebras, lux* in Latin.[3]

Another Latin motto arose later: *semper reformanda* 'always reforming.' The meaning here is that reformation is not an option for the church of Jesus Christ but it is a necessity. The church should never sit on its hands and say 'we are so glad the Reformation happened and there is no more reforming to do.' We should *always* want to be reformed by the Word of God and the Spirit of God.

Guiding principles

What I seek to do in this book is to think along these lines: 'If there were a reformation today, what might it look like?' What is the reformation that we need? This is no easy task. It would be very easy for me to 'sound off' about my own hobby-horses and talk about what I would *like* to happen, but this would be both presumptuous and self-indulgent.

I have tried to be led by three guiding principles in looking at this topic:

- First of all, what were the important, central, and precious things which were rediscovered five hundred years ago; things which are timeless and priceless, good and necessary for God's people at all times and in every place?
- Secondly, what are the needs of the church at present, in the early twenty-first century — centring on the local church but extending to

the community, society, nation, and even to the whole world?

- And then thirdly, what does the Word of God actually say? What is a truly *biblical* reformation? In what way does God himself want us to 'reform,' if indeed he does?

Let us look at that third point and return to Isaiah 17:7, 8:

In that day man will look to his Maker, and his eyes will look on the Holy One of Israel. He will not look to the altars, the work of his hands, and he will not look on what his own fingers have made, either the Asherim or the altars of incense.

Every true reformation will lead to this result: *People will leave their idols and turn to God himself.* They will abandon what their own hands and their own imaginations have devised. We can see this in action, on three separate occasions in Bible history.

Three reformations

It happened in the days of Elijah. In the ninth century BC the people of Israel were immersed in the worship of Baal, so much so that it seemed to Elijah that he was the only true prophet of God remaining. But then, there was a great day of reckoning on Mount Carmel, where the LORD demonstrated, beyond any contradiction, that he was God and not Baal. The LORD sent fire down from heaven, which licked up not only the wood and the offering, but the water which filled the trenches. And the people could only cry, 'the LORD — he is God; the LORD — he is God!' (1 Kings 18:39).

It occurred in the days of King Josiah of Judah. Two hundred and fifty years later, the northern kingdom of Israel had been swallowed up by the Assyrian Empire, and the southern kingdom of Judah was struggling to survive. Some of the kings of Judah had actually led the way in turning the people away from God. But then, a godly young king called Josiah arose, and something wonderful happened during his reign. Whilst clearing out the temple, they found a book underneath all the rubbish. What effect did this book have?

Then Shaphan the secretary told the king, "Hilkiah the priest has given me a book." And Shaphan read it before the king. When the king heard the words of the Book of the Law, he tore his clothes. And the king commanded Hilkiah the priest, and Ahikam the son of Shaphan, and Achbor the son of Micaiah, and Shaphan the secretary, and Asaiah the king's servant, saying, "Go, inquire of the LORD for me, and for the people, and for all Judah, concerning the words of this book that has been found. For great is the wrath of the LORD that is kindled against us, because our fathers have not obeyed the words of this book, to do according to all that is written concerning us."

— 2 KINGS 22:10-13

It happened in the days of the apostle Paul when he was in Ephesus. There we read that:

> Many of those who were now believers came, confessing and divulging their practices. And a number of those who had practiced magic arts brought their books together and burned them in the sight of all. And they counted the value of them and found it came to fifty thousand pieces of silver. So the word of the Lord continued to increase and prevail mightily.

> — ACTS 19:18-20

Here, if you like, are three reformations recorded for us in the Bible. What happens each time? There is a turning back to the Lord and to his Word. People are deeply convicted and persuaded that God is Lord, King, and Ruler; he demands their allegiance, their life, their soul, and their all. They turn away from those things that God is not pleased with; they turn away from their altars, from the work of their hands, and worship and serve God alone.

What we might call a reformation, or indeed a revival, is nothing less than the work of God upon the hearts and minds of human beings, whether they be many or few.[4]

How was it known in the early church that a genuine work of God was going on in Thessalonica? Paul himself tells us in 1 Thessalonians 1:8-10:

> For not only has the word of the Lord sounded forth from you in Macedonia and Achaia, but your faith in God has

gone forth everywhere, so that we need not say anything. For they themselves report concerning us the kind of reception we had among you, and how you turned to God from idols to serve the living and true God, and to wait for his Son from heaven, whom he raised from the dead, Jesus who delivers us from the wrath to come.

This is the key expression: 'how you turned from idols to serve the living and true God.' This is what happens in reformation. It is what you and I should be hungering and thirsting for in our own personal walk with the Lord, and in our inner beings, hearts, minds, and wills. But it is also what we should be hungering and thirsting for in our churches and among God's people in every place.

Questions for discussion

1. Should church leaders or politicians 'apologize' for the Reformation, or indeed 'apologize' for any events which happened several centuries ago?
2. Why is the translation of the Bible into the languages of the people — then and now — such a necessary and important task?
3. Why might it be dangerous for Christians to say 'we don't need a reformation today'?
4. Elijah, Josiah and Paul were all 'leaders' in one

form or another. Are human 'leaders' essential if there is going to be a reformation?

5. Is the expression 'you turned from idols to serve the living and true God' an accurate description of what happens in *every* reformation?

6. What are the idols that you need to turn from in your own life?

Chapter 2

THE WORD OF GOD'S GRACE

> Therefore be alert, remembering that for three years I did
> not cease night or day to admonish every one with tears.
> And now I commend you to God and to the word of his
> grace, which is able to build you up and to give you the
> inheritance among all those who are sanctified.
>
> — ACTS 20:31-32

Thus far, we have touched on the Reformation in the
sixteenth century and we have also briefly looked at revivals
in Bible times. But what about today?

Do we need to reform?

Tom Welsh, writing in the *Sunday Telegraph*, was of the
opinion that we *do* need a reformation today. He said:

> Five centuries later, we need another Reformation. Not,

obviously, in any religious sense: to thrive following our own break with Rome, our iconoclasm must be economic. Once again, we need a massive transfer of wealth, but this time from the state to the people.[1]

This reformation has nothing to do with the church, with the Bible, with belief, with worship, or anything in that realm. Welsh sees wealth-transfer as the great need of the nation.

Others have discussed similar concepts. They may not use the vocabulary of reformation, but they will talk about the need for change or for something big and radical to happen. Around the same time Welsh's article was published, I attended a Proms concert in the salubrious surroundings of a Peckham multi-story car park, in south London, where a children's choir were singing. They sang a song in which they were joined by a full orchestra and two professional soloists. The music was very beautiful and moving; I even added it to my Spotify playlist! The man who introduced the piece spoke about the song expressing 'hope and anger' — an interesting combination.[2]

Why hope, and why anger? The theme of the song was environmentalism: the state of the sea, the trees, and the sky. When I talked to one or two parents afterwards, they were also very moved. They were not moved by the music, as I was. Not even by the fact that their own son or daughter sung in the choir. They were moved by the *words*, by the fact that these children, the new generation, were giving expression to the earth's pain, an environment which is being abused and destroyed. They clearly identified with this 'hope and anger.'

In the early twenty-first century, the environment is a 'Great Cause' that many people are deeply and personally committed to in a religious manner. At the time of writing, the Swedish schoolgirl Greta Thunberg, who has encouraged her generation to take part in 'school strikes' against climate change, has become one of the most famous people in the world. This is not simply a fad or a fashion. People fasten their hope and anger to this cause. Other causes attract similar devotion: equal pay for men and women; immigration and residence rights; affordable housing; combatting rising knife crime; provision of health care which is free at the point of use.[3] Something needs to change — hope and anger are in the air!

We should not say that these causes do not matter at all, or that Christians should have nothing to say about them. We can hardly help noticing them or being caught up in them. We may very well have strong views on these things; we may be called upon to lend our voices and our efforts to changing and overhauling some of these areas of life. We may even, to some extent, express a measure of 'hope' or 'anger' in relation to these things. The Wilberforces, Shaftesburys and Barnados of an earlier generation are a testimony to this.

But we need to narrow our focus somewhat and ask another question.

Who needs to reform?

When the apostle Paul said farewell to the elders in the church of Ephesus he could, if he had chosen, have mentioned all sorts of political, social, and economic issues. We know that slavery was an issue in the Roman world which Paul inhabited. The institution of slavery dominated that culture, so much so that we see it penetrating some of the New Testament books, especially the Letter to Philemon.

However, nowhere do we see the apostles, or other Christians, making slavery their 'Big, Number One Issue.' Neither do we see Paul, Peter, James, John, or even Jesus himself giving expression to their 'hope' or 'anger' in relation to slavery. We do not see anything similar in relation to unfair taxation, or the abuse of power by Roman emperors, or any other 'cause' of their day.

No — when Paul speaks to the Ephesian elders, *his overriding concern is the condition of the church of God.* It is perhaps possible to speak about Paul's own hope and anger. His hope, if you like, is that the elders in Ephesus will do as he has commanded them, and:

> ... pay careful attention to yourselves and to all the flock, in which the Holy Spirit has made you overseers, to care for the church of God, which he obtained with his own blood.

> — Acts 20:28

His anger, or perhaps his great alarm, is the prospect that 'fierce wolves will come in among you, not sparing the flock' and that 'from among your own selves will arise men speaking twisted things, to draw away the disciples after them' (Acts 20:29-30).

Paul's great passion was for the spiritual health and well-being of the church, of Christians. He wrote his letters to churches and individuals because of this motivation. The reformation that Paul looked for, worked for, and prayed for was a godly reformation in these churches. This desire far outweighed any other issue that might have faced Paul or any of the apostles.

The reformation that the Bible is concerned about is always the reformation of the church, the people of God. What happens outside the church is, by comparison, of minor importance to the apostle Paul. So, when he writes to the church in Corinth, he tells them that they should focus their concern on the holiness and purity of their own conduct — the sexually immoral man should be disciplined; but when it comes to outsiders, Paul asks: 'What have I to do with judging outsiders? Is it not those inside the church whom you are to judge?' (1 Corinthians 5:12).

This is something that we need to grasp today! Why? Because, as Christians, we are bombarded by: an unbelieving world; the prevailing worldview; the media and social media; our friends and colleagues; and our teachers and lecturers, who do not come with any biblical or Christian agenda at all. The result of this is that the big issues which the world expresses — the environment or whatever else — are given too much place in our minds.

At the forefront is the spiritual reformation of the church, not the social reformation of the world. Should we address the environment, crime, housing, health, and immigration? Yes, we should. But they should not become the preoccupation for the church. When the reformation of society becomes the main agenda, there is not simply a danger of losing our balance or our proportion, but there is also the danger of losing the gospel itself.

This is what happened with Steve Chalke (the founder of Oasis Charitable Trust), a phenomenally successful charitable fundraiser, and a man with a profound, and undoubtedly sincere, social conscience. In a hard-hitting article in *Premier Christianity*, David Robertson, former Minister of St. Peter's Free Church in Dundee, convincingly shows that Chalke is (1) 'wrong about the Church,' (2) 'wrong about the Bible,' and (3) 'wrong about Jesus.'[4] The great tragedy is that twenty-five years ago, Chalke was regarded as a voice which was both trustworthy and orthodox. However, by placing the perceived needs of society centre-stage, rather than the timeless authority of the Bible, he has gone astray.

What is a 'reformation'? *A reformation is a reformation of the church.* The effects of a reformation may well extend beyond the boundaries of the church and affect entire nations like the events five hundred years ago. In asking the question 'What kind of reformation do we need?', the 'we' is the church.

There is another question we need to answer.

How should we reform?

Paul gives us some guidelines in a couple of verses found in Acts 20. First of all, verse 27: 'I did not shrink from declaring to you the whole counsel of God.' And then verse 32:

> And now I commend you to God and to the word of his grace, which is able to build you up and to give you the inheritance among all those who are sanctified.

Every true reformation is a reformation driven by the Word of God, by men and women returning to the Bible — that is, to the words and teachings of the Bible — and submitting themselves to its divine authority.

How does this relate to us today and what might a reformation look like in 2019? In short, we need to recover a biblical mindset. *We need to relearn how to think in biblical categories, how to use biblical vocabulary, and how to insist on biblical definitions.* Worldly language, attitudes, and preoccupations that surround us are so insistent, seductive, and pervasive. They easily skew the way we think about God, mankind, the world, and the church.

Whilst answering the third question has been relatively brief, I want to spend the rest of the book unpacking this question of how we should reform further.

Questions for Discussion

1. Are hope and anger really such unusual bedfellows? Can you think of an issue that makes you both angry and hopeful?
2. What great causes — in your community, in your nation, across the world — animate you the most?
3. To what extent, if any, are these causes linked to spiritual, biblical reformation?
4. I have said that 'a reformation is a reformation of the church.' Do you find this definition unsatisfactory?
5. Did the apostle Paul have nothing whatsoever to say about slavery? Do you think he had a view on the subject?
6. What are some of the 'biblical definitions' that most need to be recaptured today?

Chapter 3

THE PILLAR AND BUTTRESS
OF THE TRUTH

> I hope to come to you soon, but I am writing these things
> to you so that, if I delay, you may know how one ought to
> behave in the household of God, which is the church of
> the living God, a pillar and buttress of the truth.
>
> — 1 TIMOTHY 3:15

We have seen how biblical reformation applies to the church. If we want to be biblically-minded, then we should share Paul's passionate and prayerful concern for the reformation of our own local church in particular, as well as the wider church.

However, that leads us to another question. What about the world *outside* the church? Is there no concern for that? Are we blind to the great needs that span our globe and our own society? Does this preoccupation with the church veer towards being parochial or even selfish? Is our heart larger than that, and what about God's heart?

I want to make two clear points in this chapter. The first of which is that:

The world needs the church

During September 1991, I can remember an outburst of rioting in the West End of Newcastle-upon-Tyne. Civil unrest, burning cars, and burning buildings. Policemen were everywhere, and it evolved into a disturbing ordeal. I was in the middle of it — not as a perpetrator, I hasten to add, but as a bystander. It happened very near the local church where I was a member at the time. In the aftermath, there was a great deal of prayer and soul-searching. One elderly gentleman was baffled why Christians were not out on the streets, telling people about the Lord. Why were they gathered in a prayer meeting, in a kind of 'holy huddle?'[1]

We could ask the same question today. What about the streets, council estates, and rural areas that lack a Christian witness? Is it not our duty to go forth and tell the people about Jesus? Is the gathered church, the 'holy huddle,' at best a distraction, and at worst, an obstacle?

At one level the answer is easy. Of course we should be telling people about Jesus! We surely want to make Jesus known to everyone: whatever their race, colour, or language. We want to make him known within the church and outside the church — in homes, shops, and cafes. We should be witnessing to people face-to-face and using many mediums to reach people with the gospel.

However, there is always the great danger of going too

far in one direction or another. In the last fifteen years or so, we have seen the phenomenon of what is being called the 'Emerging Church' — a de-institutionalizing movement. Formal gatherings and orderly meetings are not achieving grand results in reaching people 'out there'; so, this movement has decided to go out on to the streets and find other ways of 'doing church' that seem to connect with the people they encounter. The 'church,' then, will continually change into different expressions as it moves into different communities, reacting against that idea of a 'holy huddle.'[2] This may even appear to be very large-hearted and generous: God's concern is not just for the church, it is for the whole world. So let us go and change the world!

The trouble with this argument is that the New Testament frequently discusses the local as well as 'the worldwide church.' When Paul and Barnabas were sent to Antioch by the Holy Spirit, they went about establishing *churches* — not 'church' in some general, shapeless, 'let's see what happens' sense — but churches, with elders, appointed by the apostles, ruling them. We can see details of these establishments in some of the Pastoral Epistles. This is God's means of reaching the world, then and now; he calls us to plant and establish local churches, gathered churches, institutional churches, if you will.

Why did God do this? There are many possible answers, but what we need to highlight is that *the world needs the church*. What is the church? In 1 Timothy 3:15, Paul calls the church the 'pillar and buttress of the truth.' He uses two architectural terms: the church is a great pillar or a column and it is also a deep, strong foundation stone which supports the pillar. This pillar of truth must be upright, visible and imposing; and therefore it needs a robust base or buttress.

Indeed, the world needs the church. In fact, this has been true since the very beginning. We must go back four thousand years to Abraham: in him and his offspring, all the nations would be blessed (Genesis 12:3, 22:18). The people of Israel were to be a nation of priests (Exodus 19:6), and a light for all the nations (Isaiah 42:6). After Jesus came into this world and lived, died, rose, ascended, and poured out his Spirit, the command was to 'Go into all the world and proclaim the gospel to the whole creation' (Mark 16:15).

If we gather all this information together, we can see that *all the peoples of the world are to learn about God as they see his truth exhibited in the world and placarded on the mighty pillar which is the church.* History confirms this. The happiest societies on earth are those that recognize the church as being good for society and good for the whole world. In British history, the best of times have been those decades where the church has been most free. There have been agnostic or even atheist politicians and philosophers who have recognized that by attacking and molesting the church, it impacts, and even harms, the rest of society.

This is undoubtedly what Paul was aiming at when he instructed Timothy:

> ... that supplications, prayers, intercessions, and thanksgivings be made for all people, for kings and all who are in high positions, that we may lead a peaceful

and quiet life, godly and dignified in every way. This is good, and it is pleasing in the sight of God our Saviour, who desires all people to be saved and to come to the knowledge of the truth.

— 1 TIMOTHY 2:14

A society with wise rulers is one that allows freedom for the church to function so that the gospel of Jesus Christ can be proclaimed without hindrance. This is a freedom which, where it exists, is a great blessing from God. It should be cherished, and its continuation should be sought after in prayer.

Therefore, the world needs the church. But perhaps an adjective could be added to this first statement.

The world needs a strong church

How does Paul explain this? Firstly, he calls the church 'the household of God.' A household is a visible, identifiable, and ordered group of people; they live together under the same authority. Secondly, Paul speaks of 'the church of the living God.' The word 'church' means an assembly or a gathering of people together into a single place. The church is not a holy *huddle*, but it is certainly a holy assembly, or a holy gathering.

The word 'church' is not a collective noun to describe a group of Christians. We talk about flocks of sheep, herds of cattle and even 'murders' of crows. What about Christians? Surely if you collect a group of Christians together then they become an automatic church? No — when we say 'the church,' we do not mean Christian people in general, scattered here and there, doing whatever they want, wherever they are, however they like; we mean the visible, ordered gathering of Christians in a certain place, intentionally meeting together according to the biblical pattern. They do this in order that the church might be 'a pillar and buttress of the truth.'

Let us return to the beginning: how can the church be a blessing to the world? What should the church be doing?

The church will be the greatest possible blessing to the world when she is mighty in the truth and when she takes seriously this call to be the pillar and buttress of the truth. When the Reformation happened five hundred years ago, the blessings that the church knew soon overflowed to the world around those churches.

In 1936, T. C. Hammond published *In Understanding Be Men*, a summary of Christian doctrine whose title comes from Paul's words in 1 Corinthians 14:20. Hammond was born in Cork, Ireland, in 1877 but many years later he became the Principal of Moore College in Sydney, Australia. Moore College, under God's hand, became a great blessing to the world. Leon Morris, who was greatly influenced by Hammond, said of him: 'His work at Moore College gave that institution much of its present direction and established it as a bastion of evangelicalism.' [3]

We need to be mature in our understanding. Strong churches (pillar-and-foundation churches as we might call them) are composed of Christians who care about God's truth. As I said in the previous chapter, that means we need to recapture a biblical mindset and use *biblical definitions*. We need to know the truth — the truth that makes us free and will, in God's time, liberate others throughout the world.

How does all this play out in specific areas? Let us jump in and ask some clear, concrete questions and give clear, concrete answers.

What does the Bible mean when it talks about God?

It means the uncreated Creator: eternal, infinite and almighty; perfect in holiness, justice and truth. The God who is Three-in-One: Father, Son, and Holy Spirit.

What does the Bible mean when it talks about creation?

It means that God spoke everything into being by the word of his power; that he made the universe and it was all very good when he made it; that this universe did not come about by a process of blind chance or evolution, but by the creative will of God.

What does the Bible mean when it talks about man?

It means that man is a unique creation of God, made in his image, both male and female — those being clear and distinct categories which we have no right to confuse.

What does the Bible mean when it talks about sin?

It means that sin is disobedience to the revealed will of God, and when we sin, we become polluted, guilty, and liable to God's just anger and punishment.

What does the Bible mean when it talks about itself?

The Bible is the Word of God: the infallible and trustworthy revelation that God has given us to show us how we can be freed from sin and reconciled to God. As a book, the Bible is totally unique in this regard. When the church is mighty in the truth, it proclaims these truths openly and clearly.

But we have left a most important question until the end.

What does the Bible mean when it talks about Jesus?

Yes, we need to tell people about Jesus, but who exactly is this Jesus that we should be telling people about? We have no right to reinvent or recast Jesus according to people's tastes. We have no right to say 'I think Jesus might do this, or might say that.' We need to know Jesus as the Bible portrays him; Paul summarizes this in 1 Timothy 3:16:

> Great indeed, we confess, is the mystery of godliness: He was manifested in the flesh, vindicated by the Spirit, seen by angels, proclaimed among the nations, believed on in the world, taken up in glory.

We can look at some of these words in a little more detail:

- The 'mystery of godliness' — God himself revealed Jesus to us from heaven, a revelation that has to come from God and from nowhere else.
- 'Manifested in the flesh' — the Son of God took on our humanity whilst remaining fully divine.
- 'Vindicated by the Spirit' — Jesus was raised from the dead and demonstrated to be the Son of God.
- 'Seen by angels' on the day of his resurrection.
- 'Proclaimed among the nations' — the name that is above every name, the only name by which we can be saved.
- 'Believed on in the world' — the gospel which is the power of God to salvation is a power that works!
- 'Taken up in glory' — now at the right hand of the Father, in the place of all power and authority, waiting to come and judge the world, the living and the dead.

What we want to see is a reformation of the whole *world*! But the immediate business for Christians is the reformation of the *church*, because unless we are truly reformed and always reforming, we can be no blessing to those outside. We need to know the truth and hold on to it with our lives. We should be teaching and defending that same truth. We should also be encouraging one another as we are being built up in the faith that was once delivered to all the saints.

Questions for discussion

1. Should a local church cancel its prayer meetings or even Sunday services if there has been a significant disturbance in the community — a riot, a murder, a fire, or something of that kind?

2. Does the expression 'institutional church' have a slightly unsatisfactory feel about it? Can you think of a better description than 'institutional'?

3. When we talk about the church, do we mean Christians gathered in a certain place at a certain time, or do we mean all Christians everywhere, at any time? What light does the New Testament shed on this question?

4. How does my being in a church service twice on a Sunday benefit the people in my community who are not in a church building?

5. What is the connection between churches getting their theology right, and churches being a blessing to the world around them?

6. Why is it *especially* important that we get the facts about *Jesus* right?

Chapter 4

LET US WORSHIP AND BOW DOWN

> Oh come, let us worship and bow down; let us kneel before the LORD, our Maker! For he is our God, and we are the people of his pasture, and the sheep of his hand.

> — PSALM 95:6-7

Kathy is a 'reformed smoker,' which means that she is not a smoker at all. She stopped smoking a few years ago, and now she cannot stand the smell of tobacco. Mike is a 'reformed gambler'; he was once addicted to the National Lottery and various gambling websites, but he does not gamble any more.

Therefore, a 'reformed gambler' is not actually a gambler, and a 'reformed smoker' is not actually a smoker. What about a 'reformed church'? Is it still a church? Yes, it is; in fact it is a better, healthier, stronger church than it was before!

What is the point of 'reformation'? We can approach this question in various ways. When we want to 'reform' something, it means we want to give it a new form. We might talk about a 'reformed' lifestyle, a healthier kind of life in every way. We might choose to 'reform' our house in some way, or a room in the house, to change its layout.

What I have tried to stress thus far is that biblical 'reformation' is about reforming the church, the people of God. It is reforming the church to bring it in line with the Bible itself. This is the focus that we always need to keep in mind. Five hundred years ago, the Reformers clearly realized that God had called them to purify and bring their church in line with what the Bible taught them. In particular, they looked very carefully at the way the church worshipped God. If the Reformation was intended to be anything, it was certainly meant to be *a reformation of worship.*

If a reformation is to take place today, then we too need to be doing the same thing that our forefathers did in the sixteenth century. We need to look at what we do when we gather as local churches in the light of Scripture, and make any necessary changes with Scripture as our guide. And that will begin with the way we worship the living God.

This could become a controversial question. The last hundred years has witnessed plenty of 'worship wars' and I have no desire to ignite them again. My desire is to focus on the principles, rather than the details, and begin with a rather important question:

What is worship?

This question cannot be avoided. It is fair to say that there are probably as many different answers to this question as there are churches. To say that this is an area of confusion is an understatement. We live in a society that prizes difference and diversity — a society which tends to be suspicious of definitions that seem to confine and restrict. We might feel inclined to simply say 'leave worship up to individuals, or certainly leave it up to individual churches.' This is not an option if we desire a godly, biblical reformation.

I made the point earlier that a reformation today needs to recapture the right, biblical definitions: of God, man, sin, Christ, salvation, the church, and of the Bible itself. This certainly includes worship. So what is worship?

One answer that is often given is that *worship is the whole of life.* There may be some good biblical reasons for stating this. 'So, whether you eat or drink, or whatever you do, do all to the glory of God' (1 Corinthians 10:31); 'whatever you do, in word or deed, do everything in the name of the Lord Jesus, giving thanks to God the Father through him' (Colossians 3:17). But notice that neither of these two verses mention 'worship' — they both speak of 'whatever' and 'whatever' and 'worship' are not the same words!

It is true that one of the great blessings of the Reformation was that it dignified and elevated the whole of life, the 'whatever you do' of human existence. The medieval view was that if you wanted to dedicate your life to God then you had to be cloistered away as a monk, a nun, or perhaps a priest. There was a pronounced division between the clergy and the laity. If you were a layperson then it was much more difficult to ascend to that position of being 'spiritual.' The clergy were so holy that they were not allowed to marry; the laypeople were so common that they were not allowed to drink from the cup during communion.

The Reformation changed all of this for the better. The former monk Martin Luther (1483-1546) emptied the nunneries and even married one of the nuns. Her name was Katharina von Bora (1499-1552). Features of everyday life that were healthy and normal — family, work, commerce, culture, and so forth — were restored to their rightful and honourable position. The ploughman at his plough, the weaver at his loom, the mother with her children, the sailor on his ship — all these people were serving God in their daily occupations. Today, the nurse in the hospital ward, the student working on his degree, the lady who works on the check-out in the supermarket, and the courier bringing the parcel to the front door, are all serving God in their daily occupations. God's people can do all these things to the glory of God — Amen!

However, it is possible that the pendulum has swung too far the other way since the Reformation. If, at one time, the distinction between what we might call the 'sacred' and the 'secular' was too rigid, now the danger is that we collapse that distinction completely.

In Leviticus 10:10, the LORD told the people of Israel that

they were to distinguish between the holy and the common, and between the unclean and the clean. It is 'the holy and the common' that we need to think about here. For 'holy' and 'common' we could substitute 'sacred' and 'secular.'

Quite often, you will hear people saying that there is no sacred-secular distinction.[1] Everything is sacred and everything is holy. But there is a problem here: *if everything is holy then really nothing is holy.* Let us give a few simple examples in order to illustrate.

What if every book is holy? Then the Bible is holy, but so is every other book equally holy. So is the Bible holy at all? How is it different to any other book? If they are all holy, then the Bible is not holy at all. Or what about the church, the local church you belong to? Is it holy? What if the squash club and the housing association are also holy, as they must be if there is no sacred-secular divide? Or what about the Lord's Day? Is it no different to any other day? Or what about Christian people? Are they in any sense 'holy,' more holy than other people? Or what about the communion meal — is that more holy than other meals?

So what is worship? It is not enough to say that 'everything we do is worship.' All the 'holy things' in the previous paragraph come together in worship which is holy. Worship is what happens when God's people come together as a holy assembly for the purpose of calling on his name, declaring his glory, hearing his Word, dedicating themselves to his service in the whole of life. Yes, the whole of life is a noble and honourable service to God. But we must keep 'worship' as a distinct category — a holy activity.

It is the activity of a holy people, on a holy day, belonging to a holy Saviour, and following the precepts of a holy book: the Bible.

This is what the Reformers brought the church back to: they sought to reform its worship according to the teaching of the Word of God. Some did it more consistently and thoroughly than others: Martin Luther went so far, but John Calvin went a good deal further, as did those who followed in Calvin's tradition.

So worship, as understood biblically, is essentially this: *we come together as the people of God and together we declare, 'God is great.'* This word 'worship' means to ascribe worth, and declare the greatness, of God himself. Worship is the correct response to the greatness of God which contrasts to our own smallness and creatureliness. It is also the right response to God's goodness: that he is a gracious God who saves his people from their sin. God is great in creation. God is also great in redemption, which is the restoration of all things to a new, better, and perfect creation through Jesus Christ our Lord.

How can we apply this?

Worship must be centred on God himself

Psalm 95:2 exhorts God's people to 'come into his [God's] presence with thanksgiving; let us make a joyful noise to him with songs of praise!' Worship is not coming together simply to talk *about* God. Worship is to be present *with* our 'great King.'

When a great King is with a group of people, then their

attention should be fixed on him and not on one another. This emphasis goes against the tide in our present (Western) society, which could be described as narcissistic The mythological Narcissus was self-obsessed. [2] Today, we can be obsessed in a more general sense. We want not only to feel good about ourselves, but for everyone around us to feel good as well. We are a desperately self-conscious culture and this spirit has overflowed into our churches.

How does this affect our worship? The danger comes when we start to make pleasing people our main goal — when we become preoccupied with their feelings, their approval, their comfort, and even their presence — are our numbers going up or down?

What are the danger signs? They appear when we start worrying during a church service what other people, especially people who might not be Christians, are making of it all. That is such an unhelpful distraction. We need to be focused on the Lord himself and what he has said and done. He is the centre of what we are doing, and our eyes must be fixed on him. Remember, he is actually *present* as the church worships him!

Now of course, we must make sure that everything we do is clear, straightforward and uncomplicated, containing nothing that will unnecessarily hinder people, including non-Christians, from understanding what we are doing. We must never hold onto what is obscure, quaint, complex, or merely traditional, when we can easily do without such things. It is not my place to tell you what these things are: the reader should identify these in their particular church context.

If we allow what we do as a church to be shaped by the preferences of those who are outside as we perceive them, then we will become like a chameleon, shifting and changing from week to week. Or, by using another simile, we are like a patchwork quilt, multi-coloured and inconsistent, without a single or clear theme. But our theme and our purpose should be clear. According to Habakkuk 2:1: 'I will take my stand at my watch post and station myself on the tower, and look out to see what he will say to me.' That needs to be our attitude as well.

Therefore, when we worship God, we should ensure that we are worshipping God ourselves; our eyes and mind should be fixed on him rather than worrying about other people's thoughts during the service. Before an aeroplane takes off, passengers are taken through the emergency procedure and the advice is always given: 'make sure your own oxygen-mask is fitted before you start checking other people's.' This has numerous applications, but here is one of the most important: make sure that *you* are attentively worshipping God before worrying about those sitting around you.

Should we be concerned about outsiders? Of course we should, and we should long for them to be saved. How can this happen? In 1 Corinthians 14:25, Paul tells us that when an outsider sees Christians worshipping God aright, then 'the secrets of his heart are disclosed, and so, falling on his face, he will worship God and declare that God is really among you.'

Worship must be reverent and joyful

> Therefore let us be grateful for receiving a kingdom that cannot be shaken, and thus let us offer to God acceptable worship, with reverence and awe, for our God is a consuming fire.

> — HEBREWS 12:28-29

I thought long and hard before deciding to include this section. The words 'reverence and awe' are not particularly popular today. Both people and preachers are often pressurized to be more chilled, relaxed, and indeed, funny. I do not want to denigrate humour. Laughter is a great gift; it diffuses tense situations and relaxes tense bodies and minds. It is also good medicine especially when it is unexpected. Many Christians *do* need to 'lighten up' and laugh more often.

Humour in a sermon often helps. The great Baptist minister C. H. Spurgeon was a very humorous preacher. That was his natural gift and not all preachers are gifted in such ways. But Spurgeon's humour was always contextual. He was never a stand-up comedian but a preacher of the gospel of Jesus Christ. There may have been humour in his preaching, but the overall message was always serious. And our worship of God must be, fundamentally, a serious thing.

Psalm 95, like so many Psalms, is full of reverence and

awe. We see the greatness of God in his creation and in his salvation. We are told to bow down and to kneel. Whether or not we do so physically, we are certainly commanded to bow down in our hearts.

The ninety-fifth Psalm, like so many of the Psalms, is also full of joy. This is not a light, frothy, or trivial kind of amusement. This is the corrective we need — 'solid joys and lasting treasures'[3] — not what Ecclesiastes calls 'the laughter of fools.' It says in Ecclesiastes 7:5-6:

> It is better for a man to hear the rebuke of the wise than to hear the song of fools. For as the crackling of thorns under a pot, so is the laughter of the fools; this also is vanity.

Our God is a consuming fire. His fire consumes unrepentant sinners and Jesus himself passed through the same fire when he suffered the cross in his people's place. Calvary speaks of God's righteous anger against sin. On the one hand, the entire Christian message is a breathtakingly serious thing, so that 'reverence and awe' become absolutely appropriate in our worship.

On the other hand, the Christian message is the best and happiest news on earth. John Bunyan's pilgrim, Christian, experiences the burden of sin tumbling off his shoulders, and at that point he begins jumping with joy with a merry heart. All who believe in the Lord Jesus, having repented of their sin, are eternally delivered from God's anger. This is the greatest joy of all! Yes, it is a joy that can be expressed in smiles and laughter, but it is a higher, richer, deeper, nobler kind of joy than anything the world knows. It is a joy that is deeply-rooted in the security of God's love for sinners, in Jesus Christ, the Son of the Father's love — a love that chose us in him before the foundation of the world.

Questions for discussion

1. Having read this chapter, are you still inclined to think that 'all of life is worship'?
2. What is the connection between sound worship (this chapter) and sound theology (the previous chapter)?
3. What can you do to try and ensure that your attention is focused on God while you worship, and not unnecessarily distracted by other people?
4. Are there features of worship in your church which are 'obscure, quaint, complex, or merely traditional,' which perhaps could you do without?
5. What do you want outsiders to notice the most when they come into your church?
6. Does 'reverent joy' sound like an oxymoron to you? (An oxymoron is an expression which joins

together two apparently contradictory ideas —
'it was an open secret,' 'she was clearly
confused.' Are there *cultural* reasons why
'reverent joy' sounds strange?

Chapter 5

PREACHING WITH AUTHORITY

And when Jesus finished these sayings, the crowds were astonished at his teaching, for he was teaching them as one who had authority, and not as their scribes.

— MATTHEW 7:28-29

What is, or should be, the highlight of our Sunday services? When God's people come together to worship him, everything they do matters, and nothing is wasted. They read, pray, sing, and take the Lord's Supper. Sometimes, let us hope frequently, they witness a baptism. They bring their monetary gifts to the Lord. All of these actions are important and not one of them is surplus to requirement. At the heart of the service is the sermon or the preaching of God's Word; everything else should revolve around this aspect.

Jesus Christ did many wonderful things when he walked on this earth. We see a snapshot of the people's reactions in Mark 7:37: 'And they were astonished beyond measure, saying, "He has done all things well. He even makes the deaf hear and the mute speak."' However, Jesus was supremely a *preacher*. During his itinerant ministry, he stated that preaching was his priority — 'I must preach the good news of the kingdom of God to the other towns as well; for I was sent for this purpose' (Luke 4:43) — and he also set this as a priority for his disciples, as we can see in a number of places:

- 'And he said to them, "Go into all the world and *proclaim the gospel* to the whole creation"' (Mark 16:15).
- 'For Christ did not send me to baptize but to *preach the gospel*' (1 Corinthians 1:17).
- 'For if I *preach the gospel*, that gives me no ground for boasting. For necessity is laid upon me. Woe to me if I do not *preach the gospel*!' (1 Corinthians 9:16).
- 'I charge you in the presence of God and of Christ Jesus, who is to judge the living and the dead, and by his appearing and his kingdom: *preach the word*; be ready in season and out of season; reprove, rebuke, and exhort, with complete patience and teaching' (2 Timothy 4:1-2).
- '*Declare these things*; exhort and rebuke with all authority. Let no one disregard you' (Titus 2:15: emphasis mine in these quotations).

It is to the preaching of Jesus himself, the Greatest Preacher of all, that we now turn. We see the response to his preaching in the Sermon on the Mount.

Jesus' preaching was powerful

When Jesus opened his mouth and spoke, people were drawn to him and wanted to remain in his presence. They were riveted. They were hooked. Nothing else mattered. Forget England being in the semi-final or even the final of the Football World Cup, nobody wanted to get up and go to the kitchen or the bathroom when the Lord Jesus was preaching! All four Gospels, in their own different ways, demonstrate the compelling power of Jesus' teaching, his preaching, and his words.

In Matthew's Gospel, we have five great blocks of teaching, beginning with this Sermon on the Mount (chapters 5 to 7) and finishing with his sermon about the end-times (chapters 24 and 25). Furthermore, it is also in Matthew's Gospel that we read about the astonishment of the crowds; on four separate occasions, we read about the 'great crowds' that followed Jesus.

In Mark's vivid Gospel, we see the physical effect of Jesus' preaching. We read in Mark 1:27-28:

> And they were all amazed, so that they questioned among themselves, saying, "What is this? A new teaching with authority! He commands even the unclean spirits, and they obey him." And at once his fame spread

everywhere throughout all the surrounding region of Galilee.

As we read on, we realize that Christ was immensely popular; his disciples even had to prepare a boat for him as a means of keeping him from being crushed by the masses. When he came ashore from Galilee, immediately, we are told that the crowds came to him. We read in Mark 12:37 that 'the common people heard him gladly.'

In Luke's Gospel (which contains so many wonderful parables including the Good Samaritan and the Prodigal Son), we read about the kind of people that listened to Jesus:

> Now the tax collectors and sinners were all drawing near to hear him. And the Pharisees and the scribes grumbled, saying, "This man receives sinners and eats with them."
>
> — LUKE 15:1-2

It is Luke who tells us that when Jesus came to Jerusalem:

> He was teaching daily in the temple. The chief priests and the scribes and the principal men of the people were seeking to destroy him, but they did not find anything they could do, for all the people were hanging on his words.
>
> — LUKE 19:47-48

And then comes John's Gospel, which has no parables but has the great 'I am' sayings of Jesus: the bread of life, the light of the world, the door of the sheep, the good shepherd, the resurrection and the life, the true vine, and the way, the truth, and the life. It is in John that we read of the Pharisees saying to one another, 'Look, the world has gone after him' (John 12:19).

Jesus' preaching was powerful. Of course, Jesus' miracles were also powerful and, certainly in John's Gospel, the reason why so many people followed him seems to have been because of the signs and the miracles that he performed rather than his words. However, returning to our text in Matthew 7:28-29, we see that there is no doubt what astonished the people: 'he was teaching them as one who had authority, and not as their scribes.'

Let's look into this a little more.

Why Jesus' preaching was so powerful

The scribes were the official teachers in Israel during the life of Jesus. However, we are told that Jesus taught differently. The scribes never drew the same number of people or had a lasting impact on the populace. What was different about Jesus' preaching?

We might answer that it was the colourful, vivid language that Jesus used. He painted unforgettable pictures with his words. He worked his way into the minds and imaginations of his hearers, using familiar images.

- Here is a sower scattering his seed in a field (Matthew 13:3, Mark 4:3, Luke 8:5).
- Here is a shepherd, looking for his lost sheep (Matthew 18:12, Luke 15:4).
- Here is a younger son, who cannot wait to get away from his father's home and live life to the full (Luke 15:12-13).
- Here is a servant, falling on his knees, begging his master for mercy (Matthew 18:26).

Many of us would have heard these stories when we were children, and the images they conjured in our minds have remained. I am grateful to God that, as a young child, I had a headmistress who told us some of these stories. Galilee became a familiar place to me as a five-year-old.

As Jesus comes to the end of the Sermon on the Mount (Matthew 7:24-27), he introduces us to two, memorable figures. The first man is called a wise man; he is building his house on a rocky foundation because he desires stability and strength. The rain and the floods arrive. A hurricane-force wind is whipped up, but the house stands firm. Jesus pauses and introduces us to another man he calls the foolish man. He is building his house on sand — a stupid thing to do! Again, the storms arrive and the house falls flat with a great crash. Can you see the figures, the buildings, and the weather whistling around the debris?

It is important to remember that Jesus' teaching and preaching was not some kind of 'art for art's sake.' He was not trying to impress the crowd with the beauty of his language. Nor was he trying to instruct the people in architecture, agriculture, debt repayment, or anything else like that. Why did he teach and preach as he did? The answer is given in verse 24: 'Everyone then who hears these words of mine and does them will be like a wise man who built his house on the rock.' The purpose of this parable is not to make sure that you are stable in terms of housing, education, finance, family, or health. The great lesson of this pictorial scenario is simply this: *Listen to Jesus!* We should hear his words and do as he says. This will result in life rather than death. Your eternal destiny, and mine, depends on what we do with Jesus and his words.

After Pentecost, Peter preached a sermon in Jerusalem (Acts 3:22-23). He told the crowds:

> Moses said, 'The Lord God will raise up for you a prophet like me from your brothers. You shall listen to him in whatever he tells you. And it shall be that every soul who does not listen to that prophet shall be destroyed from the people.'

Jesus Christ is this Final Prophet: the Word of God, the One who speaks and the One we should be listening to. The writer to the Hebrews puts it this way:

> Therefore we must pay much closer attention to what we have heard, lest we drift away from it. For since the message declared by angels proved to be reliable, and every transgression or disobedience received a just retribution, how shall we escape if we neglect such a great salvation?

— Hebrews 2:1-3

What is the difference between the scribes and Jesus? What is it that gave Jesus such authority and power, so that people listened as they did and hung on his every word? It was that Jesus was and is the Christ, the Son of the living God. He has received all authority and power from the Father. When he spoke, the disciples and crowds knew that they were listening to the voice of Almighty God, the Word of God incarnate.

We read in John 7:45-46 that some officers were sent from the Pharisees to arrest Jesus. The officers then came back to the chief priests and Pharisees, who said to them, 'Why did you not bring him?' What was their answer? The officers answered, 'No one ever spoke like this man!'

It must have been wonderful to hear the Lord preaching! What a shame we do not have any recordings of him! What a pity they had not invented MP3 files and sermonaudio.com two thousand years ago!

However, we are forgetting something...

Jesus' preaching is so powerful

How can Jesus' preaching still be powerful today? Jesus is no longer with us; he ascended into heaven and has not walked this earth for nearly two thousand years! But I want to make a bold claim, which is that Jesus' voice, for the last two thousand years, has been *more* powerful than it was when he preached the Sermon on the Mount.

My evidence for this is nothing less than the words of Jesus himself, in John 14:12: 'Truly, truly, I say to you, whoever believes in me will also do the works that I do; and greater works than these will he do, because I am going to the Father.' What are these 'greater works'? When we come to the Book of Acts (the history of the early church), it is then that we see the crowds of people coming and listening. They are not only coming and listening, but they are repenting and believing as well. Peter preaches on the Day of Pentecost; he preaches that Jesus of Nazareth is Lord and Christ, and three thousand believe that day, and the number grows to five thousand a short time later.

Did this ever happen in Jesus' own ministry? The short answer is no, it never did. The crowds that came to Jesus after he had fed five thousand of them with five loaves and two fishes slunk away, apart from the disciples. Therefore, what differs? The answer is that the Holy Spirit, the Spirit of the risen and ascended Jesus Christ — sent by the Father when the Son had finished his work — came upon Peter and the whole company on the Day of Pentecost, so that 'with great power the apostles were giving their testimony to the resurrection of the Lord Jesus, and great grace was upon them all' (Acts 4:33).

The Holy Spirit who was sent at Pentecost remains with us, meaning that the Spirit of Jesus Christ himself is with us. Where the Spirit is, Christ is there also. This has the most important bearing on preaching. What is preaching? It is proclaiming the Word of God in the power of the Spirit of God. It is the continuation and enlargement of the ministry of Jesus himself. We should be looking, praying, and longing for great works to be happening because Jesus' preaching is just as powerful today, through the Holy Spirit who fills, empowers, and directs the preaching of Jesus Christ to our hearts.

Questions for discussion

1. What is the difference between a sermon and a Bible Study?
2. Martyn Lloyd-Jones famously said 'I can forgive a man for a bad sermon, I can forgive the preacher almost anything if he gives me a sense of God.' Do you understand what he was getting at?
3. Is the 'authority' or 'power' of a sermon simply a matter of training or mechanics — something that can be learned and perfected?
4. What is the common link between the authoritative preaching of Jesus two thousand years ago and authoritative preaching today?
5. What are the 'great works' that we should look for and long for in the church today?
6. Is enough being done in your church to identify and encourage preachers of the gospel?

Chapter 6

THE OPEN DOOR TO THE KINGDOM OF HEAVEN

> But woe to you, scribes and Pharisees, hypocrites! For you shut the kingdom of heaven in people's faces. For you neither enter yourselves nor allow those who would enter to go in.
>
> — MATTHEW 23:13

We live in the present — not in the past and not in the future — whether we like it or not. Time machines have not been invented yet, and probably never will be! We can read about the past, benefit from it, and enjoy it. We can also look forward to the future and try to anticipate what might happen. However, as responsible stewards of space and time, we have no option but to live and work in the here and now.

On the one hand, Christian ministry should always be contemporary. When we think about the needs of the church today, we must not assume that they are the same as the needs of the church five hundred years ago. On the other hand, we need to hold something else in tension with that: history does have a habit of repeating itself. This is true in politics and international relations. Britain's relationship with the rest of Europe has been a tense issue for centuries. Foreign tyrants have threatened other nations since ancient times. Similarly, the battles over Christian teaching which surfaced during the Reformation were not new. They were actually taking place fifteen hundreds years before Martin Luther's time when Jesus confronted the scribes and Pharisees. They have not disappeared today!

In Matthew 23, Christ attacks the scribes and Pharisees with volcanic vigour: 'Woe to you!' appears seven times in this chapter. 'Gentle Jesus, meek and mild' does not seem to feature very much at that point.

Why was Jesus so angry with the scribes and Pharisees? The key is verse 13:

> But woe to you, scribes and Pharisees, hypocrites! For you shut the kingdom of heaven in people's faces. For you neither enter yourselves nor allow those who would enter to go in.

What was the Reformation of the sixteenth century all about? If you understood chapter 4, you will have realized that it was a reformation of *worship*. But, perhaps we can change the question slightly: what was it a reformation *from*? If you asked the Reformers five hundred years ago, or Protestant scholars of the Reformation up to the nineteenth century, they would probably say, in the words of William

Cunningham, that it was a 'Reformation from Popery.' That is the language they would use. I believe that the Reformers would have said that Popery, like the teaching of the scribes and Pharisees, shuts the kingdom of heaven in people's faces, and that is why the Reformation was needed.[1]

Today, of course, language like this would seem bigoted and offensive. It would land us in trouble if we used it in certain situations. We also need to be fair and acknowledge that there are many good reasons why we might be reluctant to speak critically or unfavourably about the heirs of Popery today — professing Roman Catholics. Therefore, I ask the first of two questions:

What should we make of Roman Catholicism?

In 1517, there was no doubt that the greatest threat to the gospel and to the true church came from Rome. The Reformers all identified the Pope as the 'man of sin' or the antichrist. We might say today that more serious threats come from materialism, atheism, secular humanism, or perhaps Islam. Is the Roman Catholic Church a threat to the true gospel and the true church? Let us think of some plausible reasons why it might *not* be, or might not *seem* to be.

We would certainly be quite wrong to say that everything that happened in church history before 1517 is somehow second-rate, or inferior, or of no value, compared to what came afterwards. Far from it! We could list names like Augustine (354-430), Anselm of Canterbury (c.1033-1109), Bernard of Clairvaux (1090-1153), and Thomas

Aquinas (1225-1274). We might reasonably call these men 'Roman Catholics' whilst also noting that they were godly, spiritual, believing men who can teach us so much. These figures 'knock spots off' many professing evangelicals today! The Lord Jesus Christ said that 'I will build my church, and the gates of hell shall not prevail against it' (Matthew 16:18). The church of Jesus Christ has never been extinguished in these last two thousand years, and neither can it be.

We might then say that the Roman Catholic Church is an impressive, worldwide organization. In September 2017, the news channels showed pictures of Cardinal Cormac Murphy O'Connor's funeral in Westminster Cathedral, and what an impressive pageant it was: with ordered ranks of robed clergymen processing into the ancient place of worship, it was an occasion of solemn pomp and nobility. Surely this is what you would expect from an organization which claims to trace an unbroken line of succession from the apostle Peter?

I once had the temerity to speak to a Roman Catholic lady and question whether the church she belonged to was a true church, and she said something like this to me: 'surely, if there is a church anywhere in the world, it *has* to be the Roman Catholic Church!' And if you take a look at it for a while, you might be inclined to agree with her wholeheartedly.

If we were honest, prominent Roman Catholics often speak with far greater courage and clarity, especially on ethical issues, than many so-called Protestants. Whatever our political leanings, many of us will have witnessed and admired the conviction and composure of the Conservative MP Jacob Rees-Mogg, when he speaks about abortion and same-sex marriage. Not all 'Protestants' speak with anything like the same courage or consistency.

We may go even further and suggest that there are probably a significant number of born-again believers within the Roman Catholic Church. The Spirit of God can regenerate people in churches of all kinds; we should not be afraid of admitting and glorying in this fact. Our sovereign God can work in places and people that we would often shun or deem as unexpected converts. The label people attach to a certain denomination or association is, in itself, no barrier to the Spirit of God who works in both grace and power — our God is far greater than our labelling!

Therefore, we might well ask at this point whether there is anything wrong with the Roman Catholic Church at all? Why not return to the old fold? Why not have a complete Counter-Reformation and absorb every Protestant denomination and association back into Rome?

The answer is that we need to know what the official teaching of Rome is, as found in many of their historical documents, their Councils and Catechisms, and their pronouncements and decrees. What is the Roman Catholic system? What do they actually hold to as their doctrine?

This is the important question. Over the years I have met Roman Catholics who say things like 'our priest doesn't believe half of what the Pope says, and neither do most of our congregation.' But is that really a satisfactory state of affairs?

When we look at the official, codified teaching of the Church of Rome, we find that they have *really not shifted* from the position which the Reformers opposed five hundred years ago. Look at the *New Advent* online encyclopaedia to find out about their teaching.[2] In a number of important respects, Roman Catholicism continues to 'shut the kingdom of heaven in people's faces.' Please understand that I am not talking about every individual Roman Catholic, but I *am* talking about the whole system.

However, I do not simply want to denounce. As a pastor and writer, I want to proclaim the open door of the kingdom of heaven and invite everyone to enter! We need to see the glories of the true gospel. So, what are the positive points that we need to make? What should we be shouting out from the rooftops?

Open the door of the kingdom of heaven!

Here are the essential points.

We preach an open and a sufficient Bible. The Bible is the full and authoritative revelation of everything we need to know from God. The scribes and Pharisees overlaid the Word of God with their own human traditions and ceremonies — so much so that the Word of God was almost hidden.

Jesus told the Pharisees in Mark 7:13 that they were guilty of making void the word of God by their tradition that they had handed down. This will happen whenever there is corruption and degeneration within churches. But the Reformation restored the Bible to the very highest position — *Sola Scriptura* — the Bible as the ultimate and sufficient authority, in every matter on which it speaks.

The teaching and preaching of the Word of God must never be filtered or eclipsed by the pronouncements of popes, scholars, councils, or politicians. In every church there must be some traditions, but those traditions must always rest under the shadow of the Bible; they should obey it, rather than obscuring, corrupting, or standing above its meaning. Church Statements of Faith — like the Westminster Confession and the Heidelberg Catechism — interpret Scripture from underneath, so to speak.

The great outcome of true reformation and revival is the open, available, and comprehensive Bible; it is the full and free preaching of the Scriptures to everyone without distinction; it is also that the Bible gives us a complete worldview in relation to everything we need to know about God, life, and humanity.

We preach an open and freely available salvation. The scribes and Pharisees had conjured up complex and burdensome regulations which they laid upon themselves and everyone else they tried to influence. The Church of Rome, likewise, put together a series of additional rites and ceremonies which put salvation at a great distance from ordinary men, women, and children.

How are sins forgiven under the Roman Catholic system? According to their teaching, they are washed away at baptism, but other sins pile up as life goes on. How can these be dealt with? Through confession to a priest and works of penance. It is also through the regular attendance of Mass, which they still regard as a sacrifice — the body and blood of Jesus being offered again and again. What does all this mean? The joy, freedom, and assurance of salvation is kept at a great distance from people that labour under its system.

We preach that the veil of the temple was torn in two when Christ died. This was a symbol that the way to salvation was open to all following his death. We preach Jesus' words:

> Whoever hears my word and believes him who sent me has eternal life. He does not come into judgment, but has passed from death to life.

> — JOHN 5:24

We preach that Jesus:

> Entered once for all into the holy places, not by means of the blood of goats and calves but by means of his own blood, thus securing an eternal redemption.

> — HEBREWS 9:12

Salvation is for anyone who turns away from sin and trusts in Jesus Christ alone. Salvation does not rely on good works or the intercession of human priests. Neither does it rely on any of those other additional man-made sacraments.

Therefore, we preach *an open, available, unique and*

sufficient Saviour: Jesus Christ the righteous. We preach that
his blood, his resurrection, and his present intercession are
totally sufficient for our salvation. He certainly does not
need the help of other people, whether they be the various
saints throughout history, or even his own mother, the
Virgin Mary, who is revered as alternative mediator and the
Mother of God.

We preach that in Christ 'are hidden all the treasures of
wisdom and knowledge' (Colossians 2:3). We preach that
eternal life is to know the only true God, and Jesus Christ
whom he has sent, and no other. The apostle John says:

> And this is the testimony, that God gave us eternal life,
> and this life is in his Son. Whoever has the Son has life;
> whoever does not have the Son of God does not have life.
>
> — I JOHN 5:11-12

We need to preach about Jesus Christ, drawing the
conversation to him, and pointing our congregations in the
direction of a risen Saviour. When people ask us for a
reason for the hope that is within us, we should be bringing
them to Jesus as quickly as we can. When we are assailed by
doubts and fears, we, too must look at Jesus, our Saviour.

The teaching of Roman Catholicism is full of Christian
and biblical language. Certainly, it speaks of God, man, sin,
salvation, grace, Christ, forgiveness, church, holiness, and
the sacraments. It shares a common vocabulary with the
reformed tradition. Granted: it can seem very attractive and
even genuine. But, what lies at the very core of the Vatican?

If we travelled to the nerve-centre of it all, what would we find? It is a system overlaid with human tradition, human invention, and human devices that distort the meaning and character of these precious words that I have just mentioned. Eventually, the power of the true gospel is lost.

Today, the greatest and most obvious enemy of the true church and the gospel *may not* be the Roman Catholic Church. But the positive, saving, life-giving truths of the Reformation are just as necessary today as they were five hundred years ago. This is the reason why we should always be veering towards reformation. We need to return and find an open Bible, the open salvation, and a Christ who is also both open and unique.

Questions for discussion

1. Does a chapter like this risk opening old wounds rather than healing them? Is that a risk worth taking?
2. In what ways do the scribes and Pharisees in Jesus' time resemble Roman Catholic teaching and practices, especially those against which the Reformers protested?
3. What do you think are the biggest threats to the freedom of Bible-preaching churches today?
4. If it is possible for a worshipper at a Roman Catholic Church to be a born-again believer, as I

acknowledged, why say anything critical about the Roman Catholic Church?

5. How do the traditions of the Mass and confession to a priest keep salvation at arm's length?

6. What human traditions inhibit a clear gospel in churches other than Roman Catholic ones?

Chapter 7

GOD'S SPIRIT AND OUR SPIRITS

The Spirit himself bears witness with our spirit that we are children of God.

— ROMANS 8:16

The teaching of the Reformation is often summarized by the 'Five Solas' or the five great 'alone' statements: Scripture alone, Christ alone, by grace alone, through faith alone, to the glory of God alone. These five themes were at the heart of what was re-discovered at the Reformation.

But there are other precious emphases which the Reformation illuminated: bright and shining jewels which had been buried for centuries, locked-up and almost, though not quite, forgotten about. In our own day, there is a danger that we, too, could overlook them. What concepts am I referring to? Turn to Romans 8:16: 'The Spirit himself bears witness with our spirit that we are children of God.'

Here, Paul is teaching us about the Holy Spirit and how

the Spirit works with our spirits. This is a teaching which relates to our adoption as children of God — a tremendously valuable and comforting truth for any believer. Within this verse, there are three vital treasures that all believers, in every generation, need to know and rediscover. Let us come to the first of them.

1. We need to rediscover Holy Spirit Christianity

Not simply spiritual Christianity, but Holy Spirit Christianity. A little historical background is needed here.

The official teaching of the Roman Catholic Church was, and continues to be, that the Holy Spirit works mainly through the sacraments of the church, especially the Mass, or the Eucharist, as it is widely called. According to the *Catechism of the Catholic Church*, Article 739: 'Through the Church's sacraments, Christ communicates his holy and sanctifying Spirit to the members of his Body.'[1] Historically, Roman Catholic teaching tends to tie up the doctrine of the Holy Spirit with the formal and official ministry of the church.

Now let us look at the subject from a different perspective. There is a widely-held view that in Protestantism, the Holy Spirit has also been tied up not in the formal ministry and sacraments of the church, but in the Bible itself. There are those who would argue that the Charismatic Movement — which began in the 1960s with its emphasis on the gifts of the Spirit — was the rediscovery and release of the Holy Spirit which the church so desperately needed. But in reality, this is an exaggeration and a caricature of the true position.

What does the Bible actually say? We should always return to Scripture as God's authoritative and unerring voice. We do *not* say that the Holy Spirit is locked up in the Bible, but we *do* say that, in order to learn about the Holy Spirit, we must come to the Bible that was inspired by the Holy Spirit. In Romans 8:16, we see that the Holy Spirit — the Third Person of the Trinity and God himself — is a living reality in the lives of true Christians: 'The Spirit himself bears witness with our spirit that we are children of God.' He, the Spirit, comes to us; he is in us and with us. We know him personally and relationally. The Holy Spirit, promised by Jesus and sent from the Father and the Son, is poured out upon the whole church on the Day of Pentecost. The Spirit remains with all believers for ever. The Holy Spirit is the Counsellor and companion of all true Christians; the New Testament tells us this fact again and again: 'God's love has been poured into our hearts through the Holy Spirit who has been given to us' (Romans 5:5); 'do you not know that your body is a temple of the Holy Spirit within you, whom you have from God?' (1 Corinthians 6:19); 'you also, when you heard the word of truth, the gospel of your salvation, and believed in him, were sealed with the promised Holy Spirit' (Ephesians 1:13).[2]

The presence of the Holy Spirit is not tied up to formal ceremonies or church sacraments; neither is the Holy Spirit made known only through certain miraculous gifts. No, the teaching here is very clear: if you are a Christian, then you have the Holy Spirit within you. But what does this mean in practice and experience?

2. We need to rediscover the assurance of adoption

Assurance is another weighty subject. What I mean by this is the *assurance* that God's promise of salvation, through Jesus Christ, belongs to the believer. Assurance does not simply say 'Jesus Christ came to save sinners,' but 'Jesus Christ came to save sinners, *and I am one of the sinners he came to save*.'

Once more, historically, the Roman Catholic Church tends to restrict assurance by saying that only a few elevated saints have ever known true assurance; this was perhaps imbued through visions, miracles, and supernatural phenomena of that kind. However, if we were honest, we might even say that this idea of an 'uncommon assurance' also resonates within 'Reformed' Christianity. Some might say that the majority of Christians do not fully experience assurance; it is a privilege which is experienced by a spiritual elite who might graduate to that level later in life. It is almost deemed spiritually presumptuous for a young Christian to say that he or she has assurance.[3]

Now, once again, what does the Bible actually say? Return to verse 16: 'The Spirit himself bears witness with our spirit that we are children of God.' That is, the Spirit confirms in our hearts, or assures our hearts, that we are God's children. Is Paul only thinking about the apostles, or prophets, or a spiritual elite? No, he is addressing the whole church in Rome! He is saying that this is normal and is to be expected; this is the natural and healthy outcome of Holy Spirit Christianity.

We must be honest, careful, and sensitive at this point. It is possible for a real Christian to think that they might *not* be a Christian, just as it is possible for a false Christian to think that they *are* a Christian. To actually *be* saved is not identical to being *convinced* that you are saved. And yet, we should say that assurance is a normal and healthy part of genuine Christianity; we should expect it and look for it. It is the birthright of the true Christian, not something elusive that we might probably never attain in this life.[4]

What is the character of this assurance? Assurance of what? 'The Spirit himself bears witness with our spirit that we are *children of God*.' It is an assurance of adoption: that I am a child of God and may call God, my Father. Return to verse 15:

> For you did not receive the spirit of slavery to fall back into fear, but you have received the Spirit of adoption as sons, by whom we cry, "Abba! Father!"

Because this theme of adoption is so important, Paul calls the Holy Spirit the Spirit of adoption. What particular work of the Holy Spirit is Paul referring to? *To assure, affirm and confirm in our hearts that we are children of God.* This is more than a notional or factual belief; it is an experienced, felt, personal, and relational reality. What happens when the Spirit of adoption is in me and with me? I cry out 'Abba! Father!' I address God in warm, close, and intimate terms. I am the infant dandled on the Father's knee. I am the fretful child crying out for the Father's comfort. I am the beaming son with a spring in my step, confident of my Father's unchanging and eternal love.

Notice how it works: 'The Spirit himself bears witness with our spirit that we are children of God.' What we have here is the mighty Holy Spirit of God, God himself, joining forces with our own weak, fickle, and fluctuating human spirits. Imagine a feeble, sputtering mountain stream where the water's flow is weak and irregular. That is a picture of a person without the Holy Spirit. Now, travel downstream, and watch that pathetic flow as it merges with a rushing river — a Nile, a Mississippi, or an Amazon! How much stronger is its flow now! That is what happens when the Holy Spirit himself comes as a co-witness with our own spirits. There is a confluence between my own puny spirit and the mighty Spirit of God.

Once again, this is normal, natural, and healthy Christianity. It is Holy Spirit Christianity. It is the assurance of adoption. But there is one further thing that we need, and this is more important than anything else, because it is the source and fountain of it all.

3. We need to rediscover union with Christ

The reader might say: 'But I don't have this assurance you've just been describing.' What do you need to do? This is a major question, in some ways, it is too vast to answer in detail here. The answer lies in that recurring phrase: 'in Christ alone.'

Who was it that famously cried out 'Abba! Father!' It

was Jesus Christ himself. When and where did he do this?
It was the night before he was crucified, and he was in the
Garden of Gethsemane. It is only Mark who tells us that
Jesus:

> ... fell on the ground and prayed that, if it were possible,
> the hour might pass from him. And he said, "Abba,
> Father, all things are possible for you. Remove this cup
> from me. Yet not what I will, but what you will."

> — MARK 14:35-36

It is true that the Israelites in the Old Testament spoke,
in some cases, of God as their Father. However, no one ever
addressed God with such intimacy until Jesus cried: 'Abba!
Father!' Here is a wonderful truth: the believer is entitled to
address God the Father in the same way as Jesus did. Why
is this? The only answer we can give is *because of the
believer's union with Christ.*

It would be no exaggeration to say that 'union with
Christ' is the greatest and most important subject in all of
Paul's writings. One might argue that it is even greater and
more important than justification by grace through faith.
The phrase 'in Christ' or 'in Christ Jesus' dominates Paul's
letters. There can be no justification, adoption, or
sanctification; there is neither salvation or spiritual blessing
for anyone except 'in Christ.'

Indeed, 'the Spirit himself bears witness with our spirit
that we are children of God.' But how do we *become* children of
God? How are we entitled to this astonishing privilege?

Romans 8:17 goes on to tell us why it is that we are children and heirs of God. It is because we are united to Jesus Christ; Paul's language in verse 17 reveals this truth. Unfortunately, our English translations mask the fact that the apostle uses three words which speak of the believers' union and fellowship with Christ. He literally says that we are 'fellow-heirs' and 'fellow-sufferers' before being 'fellow-glorified' with Jesus.

Union with Christ, or oneness with Christ, is what we need to mediate on; it is a fellowship with, and in, Christ. Believers inherit all things including God himself because we are *fellow-heirs* with Jesus. Christians also experience suffering in this life because we are *fellow-sufferers* with Jesus. And finally, we will be glorified, permanently and irreversibly on that final Day because we are *fellow-glorified* with Jesus.

Finally...

Certain questions might be popping into your mind. One might wonder:

How on earth – or in heaven – can I get hold of all these different things that I need? The Holy Spirit: how can I get hold of him? Assurance: how can I get hold of that? Adoption: how is this possible? Do these concepts act like three, different commodities which are only available in three different ways? Do I have to go to three different shops in order to buy them?

The answer is simply this: get hold of Jesus Christ himself. To continue the illustration, there is no need to go on separate shopping trips or even enter three different shops for assurance, adoption, or the Holy Spirit. All that is required is Jesus Christ, and the rest are included in him. The best thing is that we do not require any form of payment either: it is free and full. In Christ, we have all spiritual blessings; there is no blessing outside or beyond him, and it is not something we gain later in life when we graduate, as it were.

The Christian gospel does not centre on assurance, adoption, or even the Holy Spirit. The Christian gospel is Jesus Christ and him crucified, risen, ascended and glorified. So, go to him! Come to him as you are! He will receive you and he promises never to turn you away.

Questions for discussion

1. What does the word 'spiritual' mean? Does it help if you remember that the word for 'spirit' in the Bible — in both Hebrew and Greek — means 'breath' or 'wind'?

2. Can a true Christian be more or less 'spiritual'?

3. Is it helpful to talk about a Christian 'receiving assurance'?

4. If a friend says that they are too unworthy to take the Lord's Supper, but they know that they are a Christian, what would your advice be?

5. Why is union with Christ so important in

helping us understand our own experience of
the Holy Spirit?

6. Why is our adoption such a great blessing? Why
do we (perhaps) make less of adoption than we
do of justification?

Chapter 8

IF THERE IS ANY EXCELLENCE...

> Finally, brothers, whatever is true, whatever is honourable, whatever is just, whatever is pure, whatever is lovely, whatever is commendable, if there is any excellence, if there is anything worthy of praise, think about these things. What you have learned and received and heard and seen in me — practise these things, and the God of peace will be with you.
>
> — PHILIPPIANS 4:8-9

This chapter might seem a rather unusual take on the general subject of reformation. It may not even be the most obvious treatment of this well-known verse in Philippians. But one of the great side-effects of reformation, if you like, is its broader effect on a culture — elevating it, ennobling it and beautifying it.

Perhaps I am the only person living in the western

hemisphere who thinks that we are living in a world and a society which is increasingly impoverished, barren, ugly, superficial and trivialized — but I suspect that I am not! It certainly is not my intention to be drawn into divisive and controversial debates about areas of life and culture where Christians may differ substantially.

The apostle Paul tells us that some things are true, honourable, just, pure, lovely, commendable, excellent, and worthy of praise. We have all heard the saying, 'Beauty is in the eye of the beholder.' This statement is often used to mean that all things are subjective and a matter of one's opinion. What is beautiful to me might be ugly to you, and vice versa — there is no objective conclusion on the matter.

However, the Word of God tells us that certain things *are* true, honourable, just, pure, lovely, commendable, excellent, and worthy of praise. So let us take the line 'Beauty is in the eye of the beholder' and affirm that it is true. *But it is ultimately true only of God himself, because he is the Great Beholder.*

God himself defines what is true, honourable, just, pure, lovely, commendable, excellent, and worthy of praise! How do I know whether something is beautiful, good, valuable, or lovely? We must ask the question, 'what does God think of it?' And just as some things are beautiful, other things are ugly.

Here are five aspects of contemporary life which, I suggest, need beautifying. Arguably, reformation, when it really gets down to the roots, has a beautifying effect. In each of these cases, what we need is a better vision or an elevated understanding of what we are looking at.

1. Beautiful companions

We are often told that people are lonelier than ever today, despite an increasing population and people living 'cheek by jowl' in our towns and cities. The number of people that we know, and the number of people we could really call our friends, are probably two very different numbers. There are two particular challenges in this realm.

First of all, we need to rediscover true companionship in a digital age. In 2 John 12, we read the apostle's wishes:

> Though I have much to write to you, I would rather not use paper and ink. Instead I hope to come to you and talk face to face, so that our joy may be complete.

Today we might substitute 'touch-screen' or 'mobile device' in place of paper and ink. We might have many 'friends' on social media, but are they really close friends? Is our friendship with them actually something self-serving or narcissistic? Do we want lots of 'friends' in order that our other 'friends' will see how many 'friends' we have online?

Companionship should be 'face-to-face' or at least shoulder-to-shoulder. Companionship means talking to one another and listening to one another. Companionship means being true, as in Philippians 4:8. It means the absence of deceit or hypocrisy in our relationship. Companionship means being honest to the point of being vulnerable, but doing so without fear of rejection. This must be true in the friendship of marriage, but it should also apply to friendships between people of the same sex, which leads me on to a second observation.

Close companionship between people of the same sex can be cultivated without it being sexual. Why do we hear about so many sexual relationships between people of the same sex? Is it because people are searching for honesty, intimacy, acceptance, even vulnerability — which are good and right in themselves — but in a society that no longer draws a red line above homosexuality, and instead affirms and embraces it? People do not know where they need to stop.

Remember David and Jonathan and how close they were and how they loved one another, even with a kind of jealous intensity; but there was nothing sexual about their relationship, though many have tried to suggest that there was. Their friendship was probably unique in many regards, but the Bible includes it for our inspiration and encouragement. Perhaps we should be challenged — and I speak especially to the men here — to cultivate friendships like theirs.

2. Beautiful culture

By 'beautiful culture' I do not mean that we all have to become connoisseurs of what one might call 'high culture' — the fine art of the Renaissance, the music of Haydn, or the literature of Dante Alighieri — but that we do need to recognize is that there are categories of true and false, of pure and impure, of lovely and ugly, of excellent and mediocre, across the entire spectrum of human creativity.

I will risk one example. A number of years ago, I was talking to someone about the subject of music in worship. He was suggesting that there might be certain cultures or subcultures where *any* kind of music would be acceptable. What about Seventies-style punk rock, I wondered? Could that style — Johnny Rotten and Sid Vicious, and so forth — ever be used in worship? I suggested that this would be unacceptable.

But perhaps we should change the question slightly and ask whether that kind of music can ever be *beautiful*. Can it ever be described as pure, lovely, commendable, excellent, or worthy of praise?

If we say that *any* music can be lovely, that for some people this Seventies punk sound is beautiful, then how about the sense of smell? Take the smell of blocked drains, or rotten eggs. Could these ever be described as beautiful in some people's nostrils, whereas the smell of freshly-baked bread, or roses or sweet peas, might be beautiful for others? Or, what about sights: can what is offensively ugly to me be stunningly beautiful to you?

If we say that it can, then we are guilty of falling into a relativism that is unable to make any value-judgements whatsoever. Against this, God says that certain things *are* true, honourable, just, pure, and so forth. Because of this, we, who claim to love God need to exercise discernment and, in God's image, enjoy the things that are true, honourable, just, and pure. I do not want to set out to be prescriptive, but will just ask a question or two: What do we watch? What do we read? What do we listen to? How do we spend our important leisure time? Are these things good, noble, elevating, improving, and wholesome? Or, are they not?

3. Beautiful citizens

Historically, when the Word of God takes hold of the church and then the society, further improvement takes place across many areas of life. There are too many examples to list. We might remember William Wilberforce and the Clapham Sect. We have heard of the abolition of slavery, but we might not be so familiar with the abolition of the national lottery of the time. The great reforms of society and the ending of abuses, were largely impelled by men and women who knew their God, knew their Bible, and did great exploits as a result.

Today, we stand in desperate need of men and women of godly principle. Today's National Lottery was controversial when it was introduced in 1994, but the floodgates have opened since then: laws and regulations affecting Sunday trading, crime and punishment, education, abortion, divorce, marriage, transgender issues...

Sometimes, it feels as though we are living in desperate times; it is as if the tide has come right up to our necks. What can we do about this? We can certainly all pray, but it might be that some of us can do more than pray. We can write, or phone, or we can make representation. You and I can be a good, true, honourable citizen in the particular walk of life that God has called us to; we are called to make a difference and be salt and light.

Paul instructs us to do one thing. He says to us, 'think about these things.' Yes, *think* about all the things that are true, honourable, just, pure, lovely, commendable, 'excellent', and worthy of praise. Do so in the realms of companionship, culture and citizenship, and other realms that come to mind. We might respond and say: 'But thinking doesn't achieve anything! It's not thinking that's needed, but action!' We do need action, but thinking must precede action. This is the biblical method — 'as he thinks in his heart, so is he' (Proverbs 23:7, NKJV). As we cultivate our own hearts, we will be equipped to cultivate the world beyond our own hearts.[1]

What should we think about above all? Where do we find the epitome of 'true, honourable, just, pure, lovely, commendable, excellent, and worthy of praise?'

4. Beautiful Christ

As we look to Jesus Christ, we see the perfect embodiment of all these qualities. Paul says in this verse that we are to think on 'whatever' has these noble qualities. There can be no doubt that, as he lists them, he is thinking supremely of his Saviour. This is the high point of what we are called to do. We can see it in the words of Psalm 27:4:

> One thing have I asked of the LORD, that will I seek after: that I may dwell in the house of the LORD all the days of my life, to gaze upon the beauty of the LORD and to inquire in his temple.

Our best, happiest, and most exalting thoughts are those of our Lord and Saviour. This is the motivation behind so many hymns:

> Fair are the meadows,
> fairer still the woodlands,
> robed in the blooming garb of
>   spring:
> Jesus is fairer,
> Jesus is purer
> who makes the woeful heart to sing.

> O the deep, deep love of Jesus,
> love of ev'ry love the best;
> 'tis an ocean vast of blessing,
> 'tis a haven sweet of rest.
> O the deep, deep love of Jesus,
> 'tis a heav'n of heav'ns to me;
> and it lifts me up to glory,
> for it lifts me up to Thee.

> Jesus, Thou Joy of loving hearts,
> Thou Fount of life, Thou Light
>   of men,
> from the best bliss that earth imparts,
> we turn unfilled to Thee again.

> Beautiful Saviour, Wonderful
>   Counsellor,

Clothed in majesty, Lord of history,
You're the Way, the Truth, the Life.
Star of the Morning, glorious in
    holiness,
You're the Risen One, heaven's
    Champion
And You reign, You reign over all.

That is why so many hymns have been written — Jesus Christ is so beautiful, so attractive, and so desirable. Perhaps one outcome of people reading this chapter might be that they are inspired to write some new hymns?

5. Beautiful church

Notice how Paul goes on in Philippians 4:9: 'What you have learned and received and heard and seen in me — practise these things, and the God of peace will be with you.' Not only had Paul seen all these wonderful qualities in Jesus, but as Paul himself imitated Jesus, these qualities were seen in him.

We should understand the context of this passage. Paul is seeking to reconcile two ladies in the church who seem to have been at loggerheads with each other: 'I entreat Euodia and I entreat Syntyche to agree in the Lord' (Philippians 4:2). He then continues three verses later, 'Let your reasonableness be known to everyone. The Lord is at hand.' What is he saying? As we, believers, think about all these beautiful things — above all, as we meditate on the person and character of Jesus Christ himself — we should demonstrate these virtues in our own corporate life.

Paul's desire is that the church of Jesus Christ, the very bride of Christ, should be the very reflection of her husband: 'that he might present the church to himself in splendour, without spot or wrinkle or any such thing, that she might be holy and without blemish' (Ephesians 5:27). The beauty of Christ should be in us, so that the world will see that beauty, and come to the same beautiful Saviour.

Questions for discussion

1. Do you think that there are areas of public life which are impoverished, barren, ugly, superficial and trivialized?

2. How many 'friends' do you have on social media? And how many friends do you have to whom you actually talk? Are the answers to these two questions very different, and does it matter?

3. Do you think that tastes in music, for example, are purely and wholly subjective, so that Seventies-style punk rock could be as 'beautiful' as a Beethoven sonata?

4. What could you, as a citizen of the country you live in, reasonably do to enhance the quality of public life?

5. List five things about Jesus Christ that you find most wonderful, attractive, and desirable.

6. Why did Paul feel the need to urge Euodia and Syntyche to 'agree in the Lord?' Are there Euodias and Syntyches around today?

Chapter 9

DECENCY AND COMMON GRACE

> First of all, then, I urge that supplications, prayers, intercessions, and thanksgivings be made for all people, for kings and all who are in high positions, that we may lead a peaceful and quiet life, godly and dignified in every way. This is good, and it is pleasing in the sight of God our Saviour, who desires all people to be saved and to come to the knowledge of the truth.
>
> — 1 TIMOTHY 2:1-4

Those who know me well will know that I am quite a devotee of Tolkien's *The Lord of the Rings* trilogy. The films are excellent, but the books are even better. At a decisive point in the journey, when Frodo and Sam are being led by Gollum towards Mordor, we have the following incident:

> Sam stared at him [Gollum] suspiciously: he seemed frightened or excited.

'Go now? What's your little game? It isn't time yet. It can't be tea-time even, leastways not in decent places where there is tea-time.'

'Silly!' hissed Gollum. 'We're not in decent places.' [1]

Gollum was right. The borders of Mordor were not decent places, but the faraway Shire, from which Samwise Gamgee hailed, was pretty decent. Sam himself was a thoroughly decent hobbit, but any decency that might once have been detected in Gollum had evaporated many centuries earlier.

Of Decency and Common Grace

Most of us know what we mean by 'decent.' If something is decent, it appeals to us as being appropriate and civilized. If Sam thought it was tea-time, it must have been around four o'clock in the afternoon. Folks act in a decent fashion when they refrain from dropping litter in our front garden, from playing three-figure-decibel music at three in the morning, and from spitting down the stairwell of a packed London bus. Decent families eat their meals around a table and talk to one another. Decent people look you in the eye when they are talking to you. Decent individuals do not barge in on a conversation you are having with another person, they stand at a distance and wait their turn. Decent adults keep their word; what they say they are going to do, they will do. Decent children pull out their ear-plugs and take their feet off the chair in front of them when a grown-up talks to them.

But there are plenty of decent people and decent societies, even when they are not specifically Christian. Why is this? Theologically, this belongs to the realm of what is called common grace. The Reformed theologian Louis Berkhof (1873-1957) has a lengthy section on common grace in his excellent *Systematic Theology*. He says about it that it:

> ... appears also in the natural blessings which God showers upon man in the present life, in spite of the fact that man has forfeited them and lies under the sentence of death. It is seen in all that God does to restrain the devastating influence and development of sin in the world, and to maintain and enrich and develop the natural life of mankind in general and of those individuals who constitute the human race.[2]

Common grace is not the same as saving grace, or special grace — the grace by which God saves sinners through the work of Christ — but at the same time, common grace is rightly termed 'grace', says Berkhof, rather than simply 'goodness, kindness, benevolence, mercy, or longsuffering.' The fact that God is good to any sinner at all, in any way, even allowing them a single day of life or a single breath of air, is an expression of his grace. God 'is the Saviour of all people, especially of those who believe' (1 Timothy 4:10). Indeed, argues Berkhof, it is only because of the work of Christ that grace is shown to fallen man:

Reformed theologians ... believe that important natural benefits accrue to the whole human race from the death of Christ, and that in these benefits the unbelieving, the impenitent and the reprobate also share. In every covenant transaction recorded in Scripture it appears that the covenant of grace carries with it not only spiritual but also material blessings, and those material blessings are generally of such a kind that they are naturally shared also by unbelievers.[3]

Although Berkhof moved to Grand Rapids, Michigan around his ninth birthday, he originally hailed from the Netherlands. The theme of Common Grace is one that was studied and developed to a great extent within the Dutch tradition by figures like Dr. Herman Kuiper, to whom Berkhof refers:

Thus Dr. H. Kuiper classifies the common grace ... under three heads, namely: (1) Universal Common Grace, a grace that extends to all creatures; (2) General Common Grace, that is a grace which applies to mankind in general and to every member of the human race; and (3) Covenant Common Grace, a grace that is common to all those who live in the sphere of the covenant, whether they belong to the elect or not.[4]

Covenant common grace

Let us return to Sam Gamgee's tea-time, the litter-free garden, the quiet neighbourhood, the attentive children, and all the rest of it. To which of the three categories above do these examples belong?

I think we would agree fairly quickly that the right answer is 'Covenant Common Grace, a grace that is common to *all those who live in the sphere of the covenant*, whether they belong to the elect or not.' But what exactly is this 'sphere of the covenant'? Is it simply the church, the people who publicly identify as Christians? This might seem to be the answer; we know that some people in churches are not actually born again, but the Word of God still has beneficial effects on their lives.

However, spheres can be of very different sizes. For example, a number of nations have viewed themselves as 'covenanted' to God in some sense. The most obvious and striking example would be Scotland, where the National Covenant was issued in 1638. From this flowed the Solemn League and Covenant between Scotland, England, and Ireland in 1643, and the extension of this principle to the colonies which made up the British Empire in its two modern incarnations: first in America, especially in New England, and then more broadly in Canada, Australia, New Zealand, and other territories in the expanding Empire.

Can, or should, a nation be 'covenanted to God' in any sense that has biblical support? This is an emotive and controversial question. Scottish church history since about 1560, and probably long before, can really only be understood if you begin with the idea that Scotland has seen itself as a covenanted nation.

What about Psalm 33:12? 'Blessed is the nation whose God is the LORD, the people whom he has chosen as his heritage!' Surely this suggests that there are 'covenanted nations'? When we turn to the New Testament, however, we read 1 Peter 2:9: 'But you are a chosen race, a royal priesthood, a holy nation, a people for his own possession.' It is very clear here, as in the rest of the New Testament, that this 'holy nation' has no ethnic or territorial definition.

I would suggest that there can be a 'sphere of the covenant', or many such spheres, without insisting on a 'covenant nation.' To put it another way, God's common grace within a nation-state may, or may not, be advanced by the establishment of a 'state church.' That is not to say that an established state church is *always* a bad idea or necessarily unbiblical; it is simply to say that God's purposes of grace — both saving grace and common grace — are much bigger than the formal church structures in a nation-state, whether or not those structures are 'established' in the eyes of that state.

Christian culture?

So how does this 'decency' take root in a nation, or in any community? I am talking here about nations which are substantially affected by the Christian gospel. Of course, common grace is at work in cultures which have *not* been substantially affected by the gospel. There is much common grace in Japanese culture, for example, but this would be of the kind 'which applies to mankind in general and to every member of the human race,' to use Kuiper's words again.

But when we turn to Europe, not merely to Britain, it is

surely impossible to disentangle the noblest aspects of its culture from the influence of the Bible. I quote from Neil Postman's *The Disappearance of Childhood*:

> Erasmus, writing as late as 1523, gives us a vivid image of a German inn in his Diversoria. There are eighty to ninety people sitting together. They are of all social classes and all ages. Someone is washing clothes, which he hangs to dry on the stove. Another is cleaning his boots on the table. There is a common bowl for washing one's hands, but the water in it is filthy. The smell of garlic and other odors is everywhere. Spitting is frequent and unrestricted as to its destination. Everyone is sweating, for the room is overheated. Some wipe their noses on their clothing, and do not turn away when doing it.[5]

Compare Postman's words with those of another social commentator, this time in Britain — Peter Hitchens. Writing around the turn of the millennium, in the final paragraph of *The Abolition of Britain*, Hitchens exhorts his readers:

> I urge all responsible citizens to consider whether they wish to endorse the burial of a great and civilized nation, or whether they wish to halt a process which they never asked for or voted for, or were even asked if they wanted, which has brought about misery, decadence and ignorance, and which threatens to abolish one of the happiest, fairest and kindest societies which has ever existed in this imperfect world.[6]

These are just snapshots, of course. History, culture, and progress are far more complex and uneven than a straight-line, positive-gradient graph. But this is the issue: what caused the general movement towards 'one of the happiest, fairest and kindest societies which has ever existed in this imperfect world'? Hitchens writes as someone who is passionately committed to what might be called Christian culture. But what impetus could give rise to this type of culture, what must be its driving force? It can only be the spread of the Christian gospel itself and, ultimately, spiritual regeneration and conversion of individuals, whose collective lives ennoble that society and nation.

Preaching, faith, obedience and transformation

Let us return to Erasmus' observations in 1523. What he saw, heard and indeed smelled could have been reproduced almost anywhere in Europe, and it was quite unsavoury. What about medieval European 'Christendom'? Why was the Christendom of the early sixteenth century not as advanced, refined, civilized, and 'decent' as that which could be more widely observed in the nineteenth and twentieth centuries?

There are many possible answers to this, of course, and we could well point to the wider use of printing and greater literacy, improvements in education, the rise of science and technology, and the development of modern medicine, with associated progress in diet and sanitation. But even these factors, vitally important as they undeniably are, cannot be detached from the influence of the Christian gospel in profoundly personal, spiritual, and intellectual ways.

Christendom, of course, is very far from being a monolithic culture or civilization. There has been great differentiation. Imperial Russia, all the way through to Tsar Nicholas II, would historically be recognised as part of Christendom, but the 'decency' of which I am speaking of has been conspicuously absent across many strata of Russian society, and it remains so to this day. European countries with a predominantly Roman Catholic background, such as Spain, Italy, France — and it is also true of Germany to some extent — have witnessed greater upheavals in their political and cultural life than those where Protestant and Reformed doctrine have had a greater influence. In Britain, the accumulated godly effect associated with the Reformers, the Puritans, and the Evangelical Awakening of the eighteenth century have, it has often been argued, staved off the violent revolutions that convulsed many European countries from 1789 onwards.

The historian David Bebbington, in his *Evangelicalism in Modern Britain*, identified four strands within British evangelicalism: (1) Conversionism: the belief that lives need to be transformed through a 'born-again' experience and a lifelong process of following Jesus; (2) Activism: the expression and demonstration of the gospel in missionary and social reform efforts; (3) Biblicism: a high regard for and obedience to the Bible as the ultimate authority; and (4) Crucicentrism: a stress on the sacrifice of Jesus Christ on the cross as making possible the redemption of humanity.[7]

In other words, Bebbington argues cogently that British evangelicalism has been characterized by its emphasis on the preaching of the Bible, whose doctrine centres upon Jesus Christ and him crucified, addressed to the individual consciences of the hearers and leading to repentance and faith, which results in transformation at both the individual and societal level, and sometimes at the national level. Or to put it more succinctly: Preaching, faith, obedience and transformation. This is not a peculiarly British phenomenon: the same has been true in Luther's Wittenberg, in Calvin's Geneva, in Edwards' Northampton, and other places throughout time.

The gospel and society

True Christianity is not ultimately about the preservation of a certain type of culture. But just as the gospel has shaped society, as I have sought to demonstrate, so the society may be more or less favourable for the spread of the gospel. Why is it that Paul urges Timothy 'that supplications, prayers, intercessions, and thanksgivings be made for all people, for kings and all who are in high positions'? It is 'that we may lead a peaceful and quiet life, godly and dignified in every way. This is good, and it is pleasing in the sight of God our Saviour, who desires all people to be saved and to come to the knowledge of the truth' (1 Timothy 2:2-4). What Paul calls 'a peaceful and quiet life, godly and dignified in every way' are the circumstances, the 'decent' circumstances if you will, that are most conducive to gospel progress.

So whilst we give the greatest priority to the preaching of Jesus Christ, and pray for individual conversions and the advance of the gospel in every place, we are to see these blessings as umbilically linked to a society which is ordered, peaceable and, yes, decent. Something a bit like Frodo and Sam's Shire, perhaps. We are not yet in Mordor. We are not even near the borders of Mordor, but we are perhaps not as much like the Shire as we might wish.

At the end of *The Lord of the Rings*, when the One Ring has been finally destroyed, Sam asks Gandalf, 'Is everything sad going to come untrue?'[8] Even the Shire to which Sam and Frodo return is a blighted place, because a better Shire, the best Shire of all, lies only in the future.

Questions for discussion

1. Should Christians, 'people of the book,' the Bible, enjoy fantasy fiction from worlds like Middle-Earth or Narnia?
2. Can you think of some examples of common grace that make your life better or easier, today?
3. Why do you think that some non-Christians are so much 'nicer' than some Christians you know?
4. Can you think of aspects of public life which are very unsatisfactory; are they examples of God withdrawing his common grace?

5. Do you think 'Christendom' is a helpful or a useful concept?

6. Is it ever right to talk about a 'Christian country'? What about a Christian business, a Christian school, or a Christian family?

Chapter 10

DO NOT WALK IN FUTILITY

> Now this I say and testify in the Lord, that you must no longer walk as the Gentiles do, in the futility of their minds.

> — Ephesians 4:17

What might a reformation look like in a twenty-first-century Western world? It might look very different to the Reformation that took place in the sixteenth-century Western world. In the sixteenth century, Europe was dominated by the power of the Roman Catholic Church which held a grip on people's minds. The church was in great need of reformation, to rediscover the biblical gospel. The Reformation of Luther, Calvin, Tyndale, Knox and others was what was needed then, and it was what God gave at that point in history.

Today, the situation is in many ways quite different. To put it as clearly as possible — five hundred years ago, the problem was not that people did not believe in God, or did not fear God. The problem, you might say, was that they feared God *too much* — or certainly feared God *in the wrong kind of way*. The medieval culture in Europe before the Reformation was a deeply God-conscious culture. You only have to look at the architecture in thousands of English cities, towns and villages to see the evidence: cathedrals, churches, monasteries, abbeys and so on. Back then, people were very aware of God and his existence. But now, times are very different.

Does God matter to people around us today? We only have to listen to the way people speak about God — 'OMG' is now a standard abbreviation — to find out the answer to this question. This is my point: how has this spirit and attitude affected people in churches? What kind of reformation do we need today? I want to tackle this question in what we might call a medical or diagnostic fashion, looking firstly at the sickness, then the symptoms, and finally the solution.

1. The sickness — futility

When Paul talks about the Gentiles in Ephesians 4:17, he does not mean non-Jews in an ethnic sense, because most of the people he is writing to in Ephesus would not have been ethnic Jews. By the Gentiles, he means people who do not have the true knowledge of the living God; essentially, he means unbelievers. How does he describe their way of life? He uses the word 'futility.' These people 'walk ... in the futility of their minds.'

What does 'futility' mean? It means emptiness, meaninglessness, pointlessness. It is the same word that is used in the Greek translation of the Book of Ecclesiastes, which begins with the words 'Vanity of vanities,' or if you prefer, 'Meaningless! Meaningless!' Here is a whistling in the wind, a puff of air that is here one day and gone the next. Here is energy expended to absolutely no purpose. Futility is when we say 'It was all done in vain, this has achieved no purpose at all, all this has been a complete waste of time.'

Why are these Gentiles living a futile life? Ephesians 4:18 tells us: 'They are darkened in their understanding, alienated from the life of God because of the ignorance that is in them, due to their hardness of heart.' They have no knowledge of the true and living God, so they are walking around in the dark, in ignorance of God and his ways, and they live — if you will pardon the expression — in the light of that darkness.

I once read about a lady who sat at an old typewriter and decided to type out every number from one to a million. She did not even type out the digits, but typed them out in words. Imagine it if you can:

'Where are you up to, darling?'

'Well, I've just typed six hundred and forty-three thousand, nine hundred and eighty-one.'

She continued the work for many years and she wore out numerous typewriters. The thought of it would make most people feel a bit sick. When someone asked her why she had done this, she said 'Because I love typing.'

This is an extreme example of futility. However, Paul

shows us in Ephesians 4:19 a more common scenario: that people 'become callous and have given themselves up to sensuality, greedy to practice every kind of impurity.' That was true of the world that Paul knew then, and it is just as true now. The Bible is always contemporary.

Not everyone may do exactly what these ancient pagans did. Although professing Christians in churches will not, and should not do this type of thing, there is another specific way in which this futility can manifest itself.

2. The symptoms — the selfie generation

The word 'selfie' has only entered the English language in the last eight or nine years. I found the Oxford Dictionary definition very revealing:

> A photograph that one has taken of oneself, typically one taken with a smartphone or webcam and shared via social media.

It mentions a 'smartphone or webcam'. Webcams and especially smartphones are wonderful, ground-breaking inventions. But technological innovations follow people's preferences, people's appetites, and people's lusts. What do people do with selfies? They are 'shared via social media.' Why do people do that? It is worth thinking about the answer.

Perhaps you have heard the ancient Greek myth of Narcissus. The story goes that Nemesis, the goddess of revenge, wanted to punish a hunter called Narcissus for his pride. So she allured Narcissus to a pool of water which he subsequently looked into, and he marvelled. Immediately, he fell in love with his own reflection, and could not stop gazing at it. Eventually, he realized that his reflection could not return the love that he sought, and he died in despair at the bank of the pool.

Now we might say that sharing selfies is not really narcissistic. After all, we want to share photos of ourselves, for *other people* to enjoy. But if we pause for a moment, we can see that this is just a more sophisticated form of narcissism. Imagine if you could share selfies on social media, but there was no way of knowing whether anyone else had seen your selfie? Suppose that you could not know how many 'likes' you had received? Would that not defeat the whole purpose? The whole point of me taking a selfie is in order for me to share it so that I will know that other people have seen it. And the more people see it — or the more people that I believe have seen it — the happier I will feel. Basically, I will feel good about myself. This is just another kind of narcissism.

Is this not the very essence of our Western society and culture today? *We want to feel good about ourselves.* People are trying to create a world where everyone can feel good about themselves. This is why there is such relentless pressure to affirm and embrace every opinion, every lifestyle, and every deviant type of behaviour and self-identification. The greatest crime is that I should cause anyone not to feel good about himself or herself, and for this reason, various 'phobias' have become common currency: homophobia, transphobia and so forth. You have to listen to the opinion of a nine-year-old child on anything: on the environment, on Islam, on Donald Trump, or whatever, and accord him the same kind of respect that you would a learned professor. If you do not, the child might lose self-esteem. You must never tell anyone that he or she is wrong.

We want to feel good about ourselves and we need to hold up our hands, and say 'yes, us too, Christians, we want to feel good about ourselves.' It can happen in more subtle ways. Why do we enjoy playing on the apps that we can download onto our mobile devices? Might it be that we enjoy playing games and winning, beating the computer? Why do we enjoy winning? A sense of achievement easily becomes a sense of feeling good about ourselves. Is this not a form of self-love or self-worship?

Remember Narcissus, gazing at his reflection in the pool of water and unable to tear himself away, until he died. This is the very epitome of futility. He was absorbed in himself; he was in love with himself, and, in the end, it killed him. This is the reason why Western culture and civilization is slowly dying: we love ourselves and need other people to make us feel good about ourselves, but this is a love that can never be satisfied, and eventually it will kill us.

3. The solution — turn and see the greatness of God

We should meditate on the words of Isaiah 45:22. These words were instrumental in the conversion of C. H. Spurgeon: 'Turn to me and be saved, all the ends of the earth! For I am God, and there is no other.' What is the great reformation that we need, first of all in the church and then, if God permits, overflowing to the world outside? *It is that we need to turn away from Narcissus' pool, and from the selfie screen, and look up at God himself.*

I could very easily put it this way: You will never be satisfied with your love of self, but you will be satisfied if you love God. If you want to feel good about yourself then it will all end in tears — in futility and in self-destruction; but if you want to feel good about God, then it will be ultimately satisfying and fulfilling.

This is all well and good as far as it goes, but it does not go deep enough. The reason is that it still focuses on our own fulfilment and happiness, our own feeling good, as the main thing. Western Christianity has become a kind of syncretism; it is an amalgam between true Christianity and worldliness, in which we are pursuing our own comfort, contentment and fulfilment as a main goal, whilst saying that we are pursuing God.

About sixty years ago, J. I. Packer wrote an excellent essay as an introduction to John Owen's classic work, *The Death of Death in the Death of Christ*. They are words which have been read and used mightily since, and they reveal that what we might think is a new problem is really not new at all. Packer was asking why it was that so much gospel preaching in the 1950s was so ineffective, and he gave this answer:

> We would suggest that the reason lies in its own character and content. It fails to make men God-centred in their

thoughts and God-fearing in their hearts because this is not primarily what it is trying to do. One way of stating the difference between it and the old gospel is to say that it is too exclusively concerned to be "helpful" to man—to bring peace, comfort, happiness, satisfaction—and too little concerned to glorify God. The old gospel was "helpful," too—more so, indeed, than is the new—but (so to speak) incidentally, for its first concern was always to give glory to God. It was always and essentially a proclamation of Divine sovereignty in mercy and judgment, a summons to bow down and worship the mighty Lord on whom man depends for all good, both in nature and in grace. Its centre of reference was unambiguously God.[1]

What might a reformation look like in the twenty-first-century Western world? Let me say that my own understanding, imagination, desires, and even my prayers could not stretch any further or higher than what Packer has described: that Christian people come together and worship the LORD God for all that he is. That they all come together with one heart and one mind, saying 'Let God be true, and every man a liar.'[2] That we say with Jacob, 'Surely God is in this place, and I knew it not.'[3]

And then, when that happens, the attraction of selfie sticks and 'likes' on social media will fade into the background and vanish. We will know what the great Scottish pastor and theologian Thomas Chalmers (1780-1847) called 'The Expulsive Power of a New Affection' — a new affection[4] for God, for Christ, for the Spirit, for the

Word, for the Church, for everything that is holy. This is the reformation that we must seek after.

Questions for discussion

1. How do you feel when you hear people say 'OMG'? If it does not make you feel unhappy or upset, why not?

2. Can you think of activities in your life which you might describe as 'futile'?

3. What theological explanation can you give for Narcissus' despair? Why did looking at his face for so long bring him to that position?

4. How much advertising, publishing, and advice today is geared towards 'making us feel good about ourselves'?

5. Would you think of reviewing your use of social media in the light of this chapter?

6. Do you think Packer is right (today, in the twenty-first century) to suggest that a gospel whose 'centre of reference was unambiguously God' has been replaced by a gospel which is 'too exclusively concerned to be "helpful" to man'?

Chapter 11

A GODLY AMBITION

> Aspire to live quietly, and to mind your own affairs, and
> to work with your hands, as we instructed you, so that
> you may walk properly before outsiders and be
> dependent on no one.

— 1 THESSALONIANS 4:11

How should you and I live the Christian life? How, in
particular, should we think about our day-to-day living? In 1
Thessalonians 4:11, the apostle Paul presents us with an
aspiration, or an ambition. It is good for us to have
ambitions and aspirations. We might want to find a cure for
all types of cancer, or develop some wonderful new
technology which will benefit millions of people in
developing countries, or even strive to be successful in
sport. These are all good aspirations and ambitions.

But, perhaps, this one seems a bit tame: 'Aspire to live
quietly, and to mind your own affairs.' What kind of

aspiration is this? It seems a bit of a let-down. Why does Paul not formulate something more exciting than this? Surely, we can at least nail 95 Theses to a church door somewhere?

Paul wrote to a church in Thessalonica which was quite preoccupied with the idea that Christ's return was imminent. Some of the folk had become over-excitable; some of them had even turned into 'busybodies' — hot-headed people, busy interfering with other people's lives, and getting up to mischief. In this context, Paul seeks to equip these believers to live sober lives, setting out their stall for the long-term. Perhaps today's Christians need the same emphasis, though, perhaps for different reasons. Life seems so hectically demanding for many of us.

Live a quiet life

What does Paul mean by 'living quietly?' The word he uses here could simply mean 'quiet' or 'silence,' or even 'rest' as in ceasing from work. Does Paul want these people to take vows of silence or to become completely inactive? It is clear from what follows that he certainly does not mean some kind of passivity or 'quietism' in this sense. The word he uses can also mean that he wants them to live lives which are orderly and free from any unnecessary disturbance. He is really saying to them, 'keep your lives as simple and as free from agitation and noise as you can.' Do not clutter and complicate your lives if you can help it.

We need to be realistic. Some of us are called to lives which contain a good deal of necessary activity and disturbance. If you are serving with the military, the fire services, or working in an A & E ward, you have to accept the fact that your life will be very active, very busy, very disturbed, and sometimes, quite traumatic. Some seasons in life contain more of this necessary disturbance than others. When you have children at secondary school, as my wife and I do, it is a combination of the merry-go-round, the helter-skelter, and the roller-coaster! But the point is that we should not go *looking* for unnecessary disturbance.

For example, the life of a Christian in a university setting may, for a time, be rather hectic and breathless, and full of fun and excitement. However, a Christian needs to learn that this kind of life is not the norm. Paul is talking here about the settled, normal, bread-and-butter Christian life. We could apply his words like this: Do not be an adrenaline-junkie and do not go looking for novel excitement and activism. Do not simply do something because you feel something. Do not commit yourself to what is unsustainable and might wear you out.

'Aspire to live quietly.' Make a quiet, ordered life your aspiration. Ecclesiastes 4:6 says: 'Better is a handful of quietness than two hands full of toil and a striving after wind.' It is important to partake in the essential things of life. Make time for your three meals a day, rest, recreation and reflection. Draw near to God every day. Think through how you are going to live this ordered, peaceable life, as far as you are able.

This, says Paul, is a good ambition and a good aspiration. The word he uses for 'aspire' suggests that this quiet, orderly life is a noble and honourable life. It may not contain the thrills and spills and it may not be glamorous or exciting. It is, however, honouring to God. Paul then goes on to say something else, quite literally:

Mind your own business

He says 'mind your own affairs, and to work with your hands, as we instructed you.' It is possible that he is emphasising the word 'own' — 'mind your *own* affairs, and work with your *own* hands.' There are two things we need to see here: (1) the importance of focusing on our own affairs, and (2) the nobility of work.

First of all, we should give attention to our own affairs, to those things which are closest to us. We can speak about the 'proximity principle.' We should attend to our own lives, our own needs, and those of the people closest to us for whom we have first responsibility. In many cases, this will mean our family or our home.

Sometimes a certain amount of juggling will go on. We will be presented with the needs of our home, our workplace, and our church. More often than not, our responsibilities will come in just that order: home, workplace, church. This should be the default setting. There may be some circumstances where this order may vary, and we need a great deal of wisdom to know how to decide on our priorities, depending on our specific responsibilities.

But the key consideration is this: give attention to your home, to your workplace, to your church — and not to other people's. Do not neglect what is right under your nose because you are too busy thrusting that same nose into someone else's affairs! Indeed, when we talk about 'affairs' we might mean employment in the most general sense: not simply paid employment, but everything you can reasonably be expected to do, paid or unpaid, at home, work, school, or church. Whatever your affairs are in each of these areas, mind your *own* affairs!

Sadly, it appears that many in Thessalonica did not listen to Paul's words. Sometime later, he had to write a second letter to that church, in which he said

> For we hear that some among you walk in idleness, not busy at work, but busybodies. Now such persons we command and encourage in the Lord Jesus Christ to do their work quietly and to earn their own living.
>
> — 2 THESSALONIANS 3:11-12

This takes me to the second observation: the nobility of our work. This is still part of the aspiration, the ambition, which Paul sets before us. Your work is honourable and noble. When God created man, he set him to work in the Garden of Eden. Since the Fall, when sin entered the world, work has become difficult and full of toil. Work in itself, however, remains a dignified and godly activity; not only well-paid work, prestigious work, glamorous work, or visible work, but every kind of work.

Much has been said and written about the so-called 'Protestant work ethic,' especially at a time when people are remembering the Reformation. Over a century ago, Max

Weber wrote *The Protestant Ethic and the Spirit of Capitalism*. It has been a controversial book; many have observed that work and commerce have thrived where there is little or no Protestantism. But there is no doubt that where the gospel has really taken hold in a society, that society has been industrious and productive.

Here, Paul is simply urging these Christians to work with their hands — that does not necessarily mean that they all had high levels of manual dexterity (though Paul himself was a tentmaker) — but they were to be doing useful work, the work assigned to them. This work is good, honourable and God-glorifying, and far better than idleness, gossip, or being a busybody. What work has God assigned to you? Do that work cheerfully, and do not look over your shoulder at other people's work!

Be responsible

In verse 12, Paul supplies a reason for his words: 'so that you may walk properly before outsiders and be dependent on no one.' To 'walk properly' means, quite literally, to 'walk according to a good scheme' — it means to live an orderly, decent, straightforward life, and that this life should especially be noted by those are 'outside,' that is, unbelievers. Paul is not saying that we need to be impressive, outstanding, or superlative. He is not talking about something extraordinary that takes people's breath away. Remember: he is talking about the day-to-day life of believers.

But he does make this specific point: that we as

Christians should be dependent on no one. He is talking here about our material sufficiency or our management of resources. He is making an economic point. We should strive not to be a burden to others. We should aim at self-sufficiency for ourselves and our households. Paul's teaching in these areas is quite clear:

> For you yourselves know how you ought to imitate us, because we were not idle when we were with you, nor did we eat anyone's bread without paying for it, but with toil and labour we worked night and day, that we might not be a burden to any of you.
>
> — 2 THESSALONIANS 3:7-8

He then goes on to say that 'If anyone is not willing to work, let him not eat' (3:10).

How do we apply this in today's culture? Should Christians decide that they are not going to apply for any state benefits whatsoever, even Child Benefit? That would not necessarily be a wise application of this principle! The point is that the Lord's people should always be wise and careful stewards of everything that is entrusted to them, not being a burden or a drain on others, avoiding indebtedness to others. We are not talking here about getting rich, or hoarding up lots of money. We are not talking about materialism. We must be aware that the love of money is a root of all kinds of evil.

We are, however, certainly talking about economic and material prudence and responsibility. Interestingly, 'economics' literally means 'the rule of the home.' You do not have to be the Chancellor of the Exchequer or the Governor of the Bank of England to be an economist. How do we manage the affairs of our homes and everything that is ours? Economics, like charity, begins at home. And it is undoubtedly true: where the Bible and the Christian ethic has taken hold, this responsible, profitable, thrifty culture has developed. Indeed, this is what we might call the Protestant work ethic.

You might feel that this has not been a very spiritual chapter! It may seem to have been rather mundane and this-worldly. But we are talking here about the witness of God's servants in this world, and these verses in the Bible teach us that God is honoured when his servants live in this way.

Therefore, do not despise this noble and honourable ambition: to live quietly and calmly, to mind your own business, to work steadily, and to manage your resources so as to be self-sufficient. This is not just economics or ethics. This is living to the glory of God. Our society desperately needs to recover these things today.

Questions for discussion

1. Should Christians be 'ambitious'? Are any ambitions 'off the table' as far as Christians are concerned?

2. What is a 'busybody' and what is the attraction of being a 'busybody'?

3. Is your life too cluttered at the moment, and if so, how could it be 'pruned' of unnecessary and unhelpful extra baggage?

4. When you think of the word 'employment' do you instinctively think of paid employment? Is this a healthy way to think?

5. When you wake up on a Monday morning, do you groan or do you smile? Why are both reactions understandable?

6. Should Christians be independent, dependent, or interdependent? Or perhaps the answer varies in different circumstances. What should we all strive to be?

Chapter 12

REFORMATION AND PERSECUTION

Indeed, all who desire to live a godly life in Christ Jesus
will be persecuted.

— 2 TIMOTHY 3:12

When godly reformation comes, persecution of the godly
by the ungodly will invariably follow. History confirms this.
When we think about the Reformation in the sixteenth
century, we might very quickly begin thinking about the
martyrs of that Reformation, not least the English martyrs,
among them William Tyndale, Thomas Bilney, John
Bradford, John Rogers, John Hooper, Hugh Latimer,
Nicholas Ridley, and Thomas Cranmer.

Many others are far less well-known. One of my
favourite stories is the one of John Leaf, who was only
nineteen years of age when he was burned at the stake
alongside John Bradford; the older man, twenty-six years
his senior — one-time Chaplain to King Edward VI and

Prebendary of St. Paul's — turned to his young companion and said: 'Be of good comfort, brother, for we shall have a happy supper with the Lord tonight.' Yes, there were young men of nineteen who were willing to suffer and die for Jesus Christ, because 'they loved not their lives even unto death' (Revelation 12:11).[1]

The persecution of God's people is a dominant theme in the New Testament. There are so many texts about this subject that we could only quote a fraction of them all. The words of Jesus are enough for us:

Remember the word that I said to you: "A servant is not greater than his master." If they persecuted me, they will also persecute you.

— JOHN 15:20

They will lay their hands on you and persecute you, delivering you up to the synagogues and prisons, and you will be brought before kings and governors for my name's sake.

— LUKE 21:12

Truly, I say to you, there is no one who has left house or brothers or sisters or mother or father or children or lands, for my sake and for the gospel, who will not receive a hundredfold now in this time, houses and brothers and sisters and mothers and children and lands, with persecutions, and in the age to come eternal life.

— MARK 10:29-30

We can look at subject of persecution in terms of example, explanation, and endurance.

Persecution — the example

When Paul wrote his Second Letter to Timothy, he was locked up in a Roman prison, awaiting what he knew to be a certain execution — 'I am already being poured out as a drink offering,' he said, 'and the time of my departure has come' (2 Timothy 4:6). Paul did not have the treasure of *Foxe's Book of Martyrs* to draw on, so he spoke about his own suffering.

The apostle Paul is not only the foremost example of God's grace to sinners (1 Timothy 1:16), but also the foremost example of *suffering for the sake of the gospel* — even at his conversion, the Lord Jesus said 'I will show him how much he must suffer for the sake of my name' (Acts 9:16). In 2 Timothy 3:11, Paul gives us the briefest summary of his own persecutions in three cities which he visited during his first missionary journey, when he was accompanied by Barnabas. He describes his persecutions and sufferings 'at Antioch, at Iconium and at Lystra.' What happened in these three cities?

We can read about all this for ourselves in Acts 13 and 14 — take time to do so now if you have the opportunity. It makes for gripping reading. Each persecution was more severe and more physically violent than the one before.

High-ranking Jews drove Paul and Barnabas from Antioch (this was not the Antioch in Syria from which they had been sent, but a different Antioch in the region of Pisidia). Next, in Iconium, both Jews and Gentiles attempted to mistreat and stone Paul and Barnabas. And then in Lystra, after a great miracle of healing had been performed, Paul really was stoned by Jews who had come from the other cities where he had been persecuted and was dragged out of the city, presumed dead.

A passing observation here. We generally view Paul as a great scholar, as a man possessed with a brilliant intellect. We read his letters and we think, 'what an amazing mind this man had!' That is right. But this should not blind us to Paul's immense *physical* resources and admirable courage. Can we imagine the condition Paul must have been in, having been stoned at Lystra so badly that the people thought he was really dead? This is the same Paul who underwent lashings, beatings, shipwrecks, danger from robbers, dangers in cities, in wildernesses, hunger and thirst, cold and exposure and all the rest of it (2 Corinthians 11:23-27).

The persecutions Paul experienced were of the same type that countless Christians have known in the twenty centuries which have followed. One does not need to backtrack to the sixteenth century to discover martyrs for Christ. All you need to do is access the websites of organizations such as the Barnabas Fund or Open Doors to see the extent of worldwide persecution today. You can obtain their materials and then pray for persecuted Christians around the world. In this way, God's people can fulfil the exhortation of Hebrews 13:3: 'Remember those who are in prison, as though in prison with them, and those who are mistreated, since you also are in the body.'

In Western societies, persecution is more likely to take the form of social ostracization, and increasingly, we see public institutions seeking to restrict the freedoms of Christians, especially the freedom of expression. In October 2017, *The Guardian* reported that:

> An Oxford University college banned Christian Union representatives from attending its freshers' fair over concerns at the "potential for harm to freshers". Balliol Christian Union (CU) was told the college's student body, the JCR, wanted the freshers' fair to be a "secular space", according to Oxford's student newspaper Cherwell. Eventually the CU was told that a single multi-faith stall would be allowed to display leaflets, though no representatives would be allowed to staff it, according to leaked emails seen by the paper. Balliol CU boycotted this option. The decision has caused anger at Balliol, where a motion was reportedly passed unanimously accusing the JCR committee of "barring the participation of specific faith-based organisations" and describing the step as "a violation of free speech [and] a violation of religious freedom". The motion prohibited the barring of official religious societies from future freshers' fairs.[2]

Would we describe such actions as 'persecution'? A certain amount of caution and discretion might be needed before we apply that description liberally. But whatever the form of persecution, we know that when Jesus told his disciples that in following him, they would take up a cross, it was *persecution* that he meant.

Persecution — the explanation

Why does persecution happen? In 2 Timothy 3:12, Paul tells Timothy that 'all who desire to live a godly life in Christ Jesus will be persecuted.' Clearly Paul addresses Timothy as someone who genuinely 'desires to live a godly life in Christ Jesus.' This must be the settled, resolved ambition of everyone who calls themselves Christian. To be a Christian is to be a disciple of Jesus, a follower, or someone who 'desires to live a godly life in Christ Jesus' — the New Testament knows of no other type of Christian.

Timothy is to be set apart, as a man of God, from the prevailing culture around him. That is why, several times, Paul addresses Timothy as he does, identifying him as a godly individual standing out from an ungodly background: 'You however' (3:10); 'But as for you' (3:14), 'As for you' (4:5); and more fully in 1 Timothy 6:11, 'But as for you, O man of God.' In verses 10 and 11, Paul unpacks what it means for him, and what it means for Timothy, to live this godly life. 'You, however, have followed my teaching, my conduct, my aim in life, my faith, my patience, my love, my steadfastness, my persecutions and sufferings.'

What does this word 'followed' mean? Timothy has not been 'following' Paul from afar, as a sports fan might follow his favourite team, or as a speculator might follow the share prices. The idea is that Timothy has carefully attended to

Paul's doctrine and everything that flowed from it in a wholly committed fashion.

Paul speaks first about 'teaching' — this transcends the academic. Paul is teaching and modelling a way of life — a deliberate and intentioned walk of faith — in which long-suffering and steadfast patience stand out. The way Paul speaks of 'conduct' and 'aim in life' show us that he did not go about his life in an arbitrary, haphazard fashion. He asks the Corinthians, 'Do I make my plans according to the flesh, ready to say "Yes, yes" and "No, no" at the same time?' (2 Corinthians 1:17). He followed Jesus Christ, in his life and in his sufferings, earnestly and steadfastly.

But *why* does this godly life result in persecution? Surely people like Paul and Timothy are a great blessing to the church, and therefore a great blessing to the world? Yes, they are — but we need to remember that today, as in Paul's day, the world lies in the grip of Satan. The apostle John told his readers, 'We know that we are from God, and the whole world lies in the power of the evil one' (1 John 5:19).

To live a godly life in Christ Jesus is to bear the name of Jesus, his gospel, and also his reproach. To do this will bring us into conflict with a world that hates the person and the message of the Lord Jesus. The seed of the woman and the seed of the serpent continue in mutual opposition throughout the duration of this age, until Christ returns. The history of the *church* coincides exactly with the history of the *persecution of the church*.

Persecution — the endurance

Finally, let us look at the concluding words of verse 11: 'yet from them all the Lord rescued me.' We have already looked briefly at the persecutions that Paul faced in these three cities, but let us now look in a little more detail at what happened to him in Lystra. The passage I am referring to is Acts 14:19-23:

> But Jews came from Antioch and Iconium, and having persuaded the crowds, they stoned Paul and dragged him out of the city, supposing that he was dead. But when the disciples gathered about him, he rose up and entered the city, and on the next day he went on with Barnabas to Derbe. When they had preached the gospel to that city and had made many disciples, they returned to Lystra and to Iconium and to Antioch, strengthening the souls of the disciples, encouraging them to continue in the faith, and saying that through many tribulations we must enter the kingdom of God. And when they had appointed elders for them in every church, with prayer and fasting they committed them to the Lord in whom they had believed.

Notice these events. Paul's enemies, who had stoned him and dragged him out of the city, thought he was dead. Sometimes, we hear about terrible shootings in schools and colleges in the United States, where students lie very still and 'play dead' while a gunman rampages around them. But we are not told here that Paul 'played dead.' Perhaps he was unconscious, or perhaps he was in a coma; perhaps, just perhaps, his heart and his breathing stopped. But when the disciples all gathered around him, Paul rose and got up onto his feet. What had happened to him? It was a type of resurrection!

What happens next? Does Paul say to his friends, 'let's get out of here; this is such a dangerous place; they'll try and kill me again!' No. He entered the same city, Lystra, where he had just been stoned. And after going on to Derbe with Barnabas, he then returned *again* to Lystra, that same city, and then to Iconium and Antioch, the cities where he had been persecuted just a short time earlier. Paul appears to be even stronger and more resolute than he was before!

No doubt when Paul said to the disciples, 'through many tribulations we must enter the kingdom of God,' they must have looked at him with a great deal of respect and admiration. But it is not enough for us to admire Paul himself; Paul would not have us do that. He glories in the fact that the *Lord* rescued him from each and every persecution — 'yet from them all the Lord rescued me' — as would happen again and again, in Philippi, in Thessalonica, in Berea, and indeed, in Jerusalem. Time after time, Paul experienced the resurrection power of Christ. When Paul sensed the sentence of death, or when he felt that he was as good as dead and buried, the Lord remained his life, his strength, his joy, and his salvation.

Surely Paul is writing these things to Timothy, knowing of his natural timidity and nervousness. There are clear indications that Timothy was not naturally brave or physically robust. Unlike other boys, perhaps Timothy did not enjoy a rough game of football or a play-fight when he was younger! That is why Paul tells Timothy near the beginning of the Letter:

> I remind you to fan into flame the gift of God, which is in you through the laying on of my hands, for God gave us a spirit not of fear but of power and love and self-control. Therefore do not be ashamed of the testimony about our Lord, nor of me his prisoner, but share in suffering for the gospel by the power of God.
>
> — 2 TIMOTHY 1:6-8

And this is a lesson that we all need to hear today as fearful and fretful saints, in order to take fresh courage from a God who will require us to undergo persecution, but who will bring us through and make us stronger, in Christ, than we were before, for his sake and for the church's sake. We need to be men and women who live godly lives, and suffering persecution, endure it and strengthen one another. It is all for the glory of God and for our testimony to Jesus Christ.

Questions for discussion

1. Is suffering for the sake of the gospel a theme that is regularly explored in Christian ministry?

2. Do you think that you would be ready and willing to suffer martyrdom for the sake of Christ?

3. In what ways is the 'subtler' kind of persecution in the modern, Western world more dangerous for the church than the more 'unsubtle' kind of (physical/material) persecution?

4. Is it possible to be a true Christian but not to 'desire to live a godly life'?

5. If we are following Jesus sincerely, but no persecution is coming, ought we to be worried?

6. Do you think Paul experienced a 'resurrection' in Lystra? How should that affect our perspective on suffering?

A REFLECTION AND A CHALLENGE

> Direct your steps to the perpetual ruins; the enemy has destroyed everything in the sanctuary! ... Yet God my King is from of old, working salvation in the midst of the earth.
>
> — Psalm 74:3, 12

I want to end this book on a somewhat sober note, because we are living in times that are very sobering for all who love the church of our Lord and Saviour Jesus Christ. The process of writing this fairly short book has been quite long, certainly long enough for the general spiritual and moral condition of the United Kingdom and many other parts of the world to deteriorate noticeably. At least, that is my perception.

I invite the reader to turn to Psalm 74. It is a Psalm of two halves. The first half of the Psalm, up to verse 11, resembles the Book of Lamentations and indeed, it does appear likely that the Psalm was written after the destruction of Jerusalem, at the hands of the armies of Nebuchadnezzar in 587BC.

The Psalmist is observing Jerusalem and its centrepiece, the temple. It lies in a ruined state and his heart is desperately broken. Where there was once order, structure, purpose and beauty, he now sees destruction, devastation, ruin, and chaos. He does not mince his words as he describes the scene of utter desolation that confronts him: he speaks in verse 3 of the 'perpetual ruin' and the way in which 'the enemy has destroyed everything in the sanctuary.'

For us, two thousand years later, the depth of the Psalmist's despair might seem extreme. Yes, it is a terrible shame that so beautiful a building as the temple was mutilated as it was, but surely, at the end of the day, it was only a building? If a criminal gang, or a group of terrorists, were to torch St. Paul's Cathedral, or Westminster Abbey, or Durham Cathedral, we would all lament that one of our great national heritage sites had been damaged beyond repair, but we might not go as far as to say that the cause of God himself had been assailed so deeply.

But the temple in Jerusalem was far more than Israel's National Heritage Site Number One. It was, as verse 7 tells us, 'the dwelling place of your [God's] name'. It was the visible manifestation of God's covenant and salvation in the whole earth. And what the temple was back then, the church of Jesus Christ is today — the church, I must emphasize, not as a building or a number of buildings, but as *the people of God*: the people called by God to worship him and make him known in the world as the gospel of Jesus Christ is proclaimed.

As the armies of Nebuchadnezzar did great violence to the temple of God in Jerusalem long ago, so the enemies of God and of his people do great violence to the church of God today. Who are these enemies? The devil, to be sure, is one of them, stirring up hatred against the church of Jesus Christ, whilst knowing that he is defeated and doomed. The world, of course, is another enemy of the church; it persecutes God's people in both subtle and unsubtle ways, as we have seen in the previous chapter. But the third enemy is sin itself, and by this I mean the sin that remains in God's people. Tragically, great damage is done to the church by those who identify with the church, but whose motives and aims are destructive as far as the health of the church is concerned. It is principally because of these enemies that the church, in every age, stands in need of reformation.

How do these enemies attack God's church? They do so by disrupting the order and structure which God has set in place, and something of this fixed order is seen in verse 12 to 17. It is God who established humanity as male and female, and who ordained marriage. God appointed six days of work and a day of rest. God made the seasons of the year and ensured that they would continue throughout the lifetime of this earth. God put in place lawful government and authority. He set the boundaries of the nations. And he appointed his own people, the church, to be a people for his own holy possession.

The enemies of God seek to lay waste to everything that God has ordered. Where order and structure have been established, muddle, chaos and confusion are brought in. Perhaps the most signal evidence of this, today in 2020, is the confusion which relates to sexual identity and practice: the pressure witnessed in many churches to embrace and affirm same-sex practice, bisexual practice, and transgender identity — a pressure which is causing many churches, even those that have been historically orthodox and evangelical, to cave in.[1]

However, this Psalm is not an unending lamentation. The tide turns from verse 12, where the Psalmist remembers that 'God my King is from of old, working salvation in the midst of the earth.' The God who made the earth will not simply sit back, so to speak, as he watches the gradual disintegration of everything he has so lovingly and wisely created. The second half of the Psalm reaches a climax with the bold outburst in verse 20, where the Psalmist urges the LORD, 'Arise O God, defend your cause; remember how the foolish scoff at you all the day!'

This is a clarion call to the people of God — when we see the hand of our enemies against us, and against the cause of God, we are to cry out to God, to arouse him to action, so to speak, for the sake of his own name. It is not that God is inactive until his people address him in this way. But when his people see the destruction and desecration of those things that God has called holy — as in 587BC and as in 2019AD — then is the time to lift up our voices and ask God to act in his unchanging power.

There are no questions to conclude this final section of

the book. Instead, my request is a simple one: will you pray, and urge others to pray? Will you pray as a church? Will you pray especially for the church — your own local church and for the church in our nation and beyond?

Because we need a reformation today.

NOTES

Introduction

1. J. H. Merle d'Aubigné, *The Reformation in England, Volume 1* (Edinburgh: Banner of Truth, 1994), p. 23.

1. Look to our Maker

1. William Cunningham, *The Reformers and the Theology of the Reformation*, (Edinburgh: Banner of Truth), 1989, p. 1. By 'uninspired men' Cunningham does not mean that Luther, Calvin and others were boring or lacklustre, but that unlike the prophets and apostles, they did not write under the direct influence of the Holy Spirit (2 Timothy 3:16).
2. Sourced at https://www.theguardian.com/world/2016/oct/29/reformation-luther-pope-francis-catholics
3. Mike Reeves, from a 2017 address given under the auspices of Ligonier Ministries. It can be read (and viewed) at https://www.ligonier.org/learn/conferences/next-500-years-2017-national-conference/after-darkness-light/
4. Much could be written about the distinction between a 'reformation' and a 'revival,' but it will not be addressed in this book. It is sufficient to note that both a 'reformation' and a 'revival' are brought about by the sovereign and gracious work of God in history, when he turns people's hearts back to himself.

2. The word of God's grace

1. Tom Welsh, *Sunday Telegraph*, 27 August 2017, sourced at

https://www.telegraph.co.uk/news/2017/08/27/five-hundred-years-martin-luther-britain-needs-economic-reformation/

2. The song was by Kate Whitley, entitled *I Am, I Say*. Kate Whitley co-founded the Multi-Story Orchestra.

3. These are a representative sample which are still current as this book is going to press, and are reflective of the Inner London culture which surrounds me.

4. The article can be read at https://www.premierchristianity.com/Blog/Steve-Chalke-s-rethink-of-the-Bible-isn-t-just-wrong-it-s-anti-Christ.

3. The pillar and buttress of the truth

1. The term 'holy huddle' was intended in a pejorative sense.

2. That is not to say that there is no space for creativity and flexibility for a church to decide how it is going to function in relation to specific aspects of its work and ministry. For example, a church made up largely of immigrants may look, sound, and feel very different to a church in a village where the inhabitants hardly ever meet anyone from overseas. But these social and cultural considerations must take second place to the far bigger questions: what is the church, and what must the church do?

3. Quoted from an article by Paul Brown in the *Evangelical Times*, November 2011. This can be read at https://www.evangelical-times.org/23257/t-c-hammond-1877-1961/

4. Let us worship and bow down

1. This claim is often based on the frequently-quoted words of Abraham Kuyper (1837-1920), the most distinguished Dutch theologian and politician: 'There is not a square inch in the whole domain of our human existence over which Christ, who is Sovereign over all, does not cry, Mine!' But the ownership of Christ over the whole creation does not mean — at least it does not *yet* mean (Rev. 21:22!) — that this *present* world is 'holy' in a biblical sense.

2. We will look a bit more closely at Narcissus in chapter 10.

3. This expression comes John Newton's hymn *Glorious things of Thee are spoken*, and Newton (1725-1807) was certainly no sour-faced kill-joy, as anyone who reads his letters will find out.

6. The open door to the kingdom of heaven

1. John Calvin himself commented on this Matthew 23:12: 'In like manner, heaven is shut by Popery against the wretched people, while the very pastors—or, at least, those who hold that office—prevent them by their tyranny from being opened. If we are not excessively indifferent, we will not willingly enter into a league with wicked tyrants, who cruelly shut against us the entrance into life.' (Calvin, *Harmony of the Gospels Volume 3*, AGES Software, p. 62.)

2. http://www.newadvent.org/

7. God's Spirit and our spirits

1. See http://www.vatican.va/archive/ENG0015/_P24.HTM

2. We should notice that the indwelling Spirit functions both in an individual sense, as in 1 Corinthians 6:19, and also in a corporate sense, as in 1 Corinthians 3:16. We must distinguish between these two cases, although they are both part of the Spirit's indwelling.

3. I have come across this pastoral problem very frequently; most often it reveals itself in attitudes towards the Communion – 'I'm not a good enough/holy enough/knowledgeable enough Christian to come to the table.' 'But are you a Christian?' 'Yes!' 'So what is stopping you from coming?' 'I'm not a good enough/holy enough/knowledgeable enough Christian to come to the table.' And so on.

4. For an excellent treatment of this subject, see Joel R. Beeke, *The Quest for Full Assurance: the Legacy of Calvin and His Successors* (Edinburgh: Banner of Truth, 1999).

8. If there is any excellence…

1. Observe such book titles as *You are what you eat* (Gillian McKeith), *You are what you think* (David Stoop), *You are what you love* (James K. A. Smith)!

9. Decency and Common Grace

1. J. R. R. Tolkien, *The Two Towers* (London: Folio Society, 1977), p. 326.
2. Louis Berkhof, *Systematic Theology*, (Edinburgh: Banner of Truth, 1988)p. 435.
3. Berkhof, p. 438.
4. Berkhof, p. 434-5, emphasis mine.
5. Neil Postman, *The Disappearance of Childhood* (New York Vintage Books, 1994), p. 16.
6. Peter Hitchens, *The Abolition of Britain* (London: Quartet Books, 2000), p. 369.
7. David W. Bebbington, *Evangelicalism in Modern Britain: A history from the 1730s to the 1980s* (London: Routledge, 1989), p.4f.
8. J. R. R. Tolkien, *The Return of the King* (London: Folio Society, 1977), p. 242.

10. Do not walk in futility

1. J. I. Packer, 'Introductory Essay to *The Death of Death in the Death of Christ*' (Edinburgh: Banner of Truth, 1989), pp. 1-2. Packer wrote these words in 1959 and, when I first read these words in 1995, it caused such a shift in my thinking as seismic as anything else I have ever read since.
2. Romans 3:4.
3. Genesis 28:16.
4. We might substitute, in place of the word 'affection' a word such as desire or longing or enjoyment or pleasure or delight.

12. Reformation and Persecution

1. The full story of John Leaf, told by John Foxe, can be read at https://www.exclassics.com/foxe/foxe295.htm
2. https://www.theguardian.com/education/2017/oct/09/anger-as-oxford-college-bans-christian-group-from-freshers-fair

A REFLECTION AND A CHALLENGE

1. For an example of this, view this report on the All One Body Conference in a Christian Reformed Church in Grand Rapids. This is from the *Aquila Report*, 19 November 2018: https://www.theaquilareport.com/turning-the-crc-into-an-lgbtq-ally